Three Minutes a Day

VOLUME 50

THREE MINUTES A DAY
VOLUME 50

Tony Rossi
Editor-in-Chief

Gerald M. Costello
Contributing Editor

The Christophers
5 Hanover Square
New York, NY 10004

www.christophers.org

Lord, make me an instrument of Your peace.
Where there is hatred, let me sow love;
where there is injury, pardon;
where there is doubt, faith;
where there is despair, hope;
where there is darkness, light;
and where there is sadness, joy.

O Divine Master, grant that I may not so much seek
to be consoled as to console;
to be understood as to understand;
to be loved as to love.
For it is in giving that we receive;
it is in pardoning that we are pardoned;
and it is in dying that we are born to eternal life.
Amen.

PRAYER OF ST. FRANCIS
(ADOPTED AS THE PRAYER OF THE CHRISTOPHERS)

The Christophers warmly thank
all our friends, sponsors and supporters
who have made this 50th volume of
Three Minutes a Day possible.

Contributing Writers

Tony Rossi

Gerald M. Costello

Sarah E. Holinski

Joan Bromfield

Garan Santicola

Dear Friend,

It seems fitting that we are presenting Volume 50 of *Three Minutes a Day* on the heels of the 70th anniversary year of our organization in 2015. We invite all our Christopher friends to join us in celebrating this milestone publication by delving into the stories contained within these pages, stories that give renewed attention to our shared mission of lighting candles that illuminate the darkness.

The Christophers' simple but profound message about the importance of each individual in God's plan has been transforming people's lives ever since our founding in 1945 by Maryknoll Father James Keller. Through our many programs and outreaches, we highlight people who choose to see a purpose in the circumstances of their lives, and act to make a positive difference in the world around them. To all those we serve on the front lines of some of the toughest ministries, especially our prison chaplains, these stories offer a starting point to open the hearts of those in need of a fresh outlook.

Each page of this book greets us on a new day with food for thought that can lead to long-term spiritual nourishment. We hope everyone will dedicate a few brief moments daily to sit with this book and be nourished. A special thank you for the generous support of our Christopher friends who make *Three Minutes a Day* possible. God bless you!

Mary Ellen Robinson, Vice President
Father Jonathan Morris
Father Dennis W. Cleary, M.M.

I Am the New Year

Bible Illustrator magazine once published a reflection about the potential for change that a new year brings.

It read, "I am the new year. I am an unspoiled page in your book of time. I am your next chance at the art of living. I am your opportunity to practice what you have learned about life during the last twelve months.

"All that you sought and didn't find is hidden in me, waiting for you to search it but with more determination.

"All the good that you tried for and didn't achieve is mine to grant when you have fewer conflicting desires. All that you dreamed but didn't dare to do, all that you hoped for but did not will, all the faith that you claimed but did not have—these slumber lightly, waiting to be awakened by the touch of a strong purpose.

"I am your opportunity to renew your allegiance to Him who said, 'Behold, I make all things new.'"

If anyone is in Christ, there is a new creation: everything old has passed away; see, everything has become new! (2 Corinthians 5:17)

Guide me in making wise choices this new year, Father.

The Empowerment Plan

When Veronika Scott was a student at Detroit's College for Creative Studies, a teacher gave her class the assignment to create a product that fulfills a social need. With an interest in helping the homeless, Scott regularly visited a local shelter to determine what that could be.

As reported by *PBS Newshour*, "The final design was a coat that transformed into a sleeping bag," made with fabrics that would keep people warm and dry. Though it took some trial and error, the product was a success and led Scott to launch her own non-profit business called The Empowerment Plan.

She now employs 10 formerly homeless women, who have made more than 1,000 coats that have been distributed to the homeless nationwide. Elisha Carpenter, a mother of three whose wages from working with Scott allowed her to pay for housing, said, "What I really like most about the job is the sincerity of Ms. Scott because she reaches into the cesspool of homelessness and transitional housing, and she's steadily pulling people out."

Whoever is kind to the poor lends to the Lord, and will be repaid in full. (Proverbs 19:17)

How can I use my initiative to help others in need, Lord?

When a Star-Lord Prays

Actor Chris Pratt may have played the Marvel comic book hero Star-Lord in the blockbuster movie *Guardians of the Galaxy*, but his personal life is centered around a different Lord.

In 2012, Pratt's wife, actress Anna Faris, gave birth to their first child, Jack, nine weeks early. Jack was required to stay in the intensive care unit, and doctors said he might wind up suffering from various health problems.

Pratt cherished every second he spent with his son because they weren't sure he would even survive. "We were scared for a long time," he told *People* magazine. "We prayed a lot."

Thankfully, Jack improved and is now a healthy three-year-old. The whole experience, said Pratt, "restored my faith in God, not that it needed to be restored, but it really redefined it. The baby was so beautiful to us, and I look back at the photos of him and it must have been jarring for other people to come in and see him, but to us he was so beautiful and perfect."

My grace is sufficient for you, for power is made perfect in weakness. (2 Corinthians 12:9)

When my faith in You wavers, Lord, help me redefine it and make my way back to You.

When We Forgive...

Forgiving those who have hurt us is one of the most challenging but necessary decisions we can make in this life. The late priest and author Henri Nouwen offered the following reflection to make choosing forgiveness just a little bit easier:

"Forgiving does not mean forgetting. When we forgive a person, the memory of the wound might stay with us for a long time, even throughout our lives. Sometimes we carry the memory in our bodies as a visible sign. But forgiveness changes the way we remember. It converts the curse into a blessing.

"When we forgive our parents for their divorce, our children for their lack of attention, our friends for their unfaithfulness in crisis, our doctors for their ill advice, we no longer have to experience ourselves as the victims of events we had no control over. Forgiveness allows us to claim our own power and not let these events destroy us; it enables them to become events that deepen the wisdom of our hearts. Forgiveness indeed heals memories."

Forgive the iniquity of this people according to the greatness of Your steadfast love. (Numbers 14:19)

Help me cast off the burden of old resentments, Father.

The Shoplifter's Second Chance

In September 2013, unemployed mother of three Jessica Robles attempted to steal $300 worth of groceries from a Publix Super Market in Miami, but was caught before she could get away. Police Officer Vicki Thomas arrived at the scene and asked Robles her reason for shoplifting.

She responded that she did it to feed her three kids. Instead of taking her to jail, the kindhearted cop gave her a notice to appear in court on a misdemeanor charge. Officer Thomas then used $100 of her own money to buy groceries for Robles's family. She delivered them herself and witnessed the joy on the children's faces that they actually had something to eat.

When the story spread, another $700 was donated for the Robles's food expenses. And, as reported by TV station *WSVN,* a local business owner soon hired Robles for a job.

Through tears, Robles expressed her gratitude for Officer Thomas's actions, which gave her a new chance at life.

A generous person will be enriched.
(Proverbs 11:25)

Sometimes people make poor decisions, Lord. Help them realize their error and give them a chance to do right.

A Smile is an Act of Mercy

Tara and her one-year-old daughter went to visit her great-grandparents at their nursing home. She could see on the faces of the elderly couple the joy that her visit brought them.

On her way home, Tara listened to *The Jennifer Fulwiler Show* on Sirius-XM's Catholic Channel radio station and heard Christopher Award-winning author Kerry Weber being interviewed about her book *Mercy in the City*. The conversation prompted Tara to reflect on the idea of mercy, so she shared the following thoughts on her Instagram page:

"Sometimes the corporal works of mercy don't look like we expect. Visiting the imprisoned doesn't always mean visiting those in jail. Sometimes the imprisoned are those imprisoned by their bodies, unable to...do the things they want [to do]. Sometimes the imprisoned are those who receive no visitors from the outside world. Sometimes your daughter offering a smile to the elderly and the infirm can teach you more about love and mercy than years of theology. Opportunities for mercy abound in our lives, if only we take the time to see them."

He makes room for every act of mercy. (Sirach 16:14)

May I be a source of joy to the elderly and infirm, Lord.

A Groom's Unusual Vows

A husband reciting vows to his bride on their wedding day isn't unusual. But NASCAR driver Brian Scott also professed vows to his four-year-old stepdaughter Brielle.

Scott married Whitney Kay in 2014 and wanted Brielle to know that she would always be a vital part of their new life together. He therefore wrote and read the following vows:

"I promise to always hold your hand and skip with you down the street, to bring comfort to your life. I vow to make you say your prayers before you eat. I promise to read you stories at night, to always tuck you in real tight. I vow to show you how a man should treat a woman in my relationship with your mother. And above all else, I vow to protect you, care for you and love you forever."

The Scotts were surprised that the video of the vows went viral a full year after their wedding. Still, Whitney hopes it will "bring hope to anyone who feels hopeless" and remind them that "God has a beautiful plan for everyone."

Set the believers an example in speech and conduct, in love, in faith, in purity.
(1 Timothy 4:12)

Strengthen the hands and hearts of all fathers, Creator.

Is Anything Really Missing?

Shel Silverstein tells a story called *The Missing Piece*. A circle was missing a wedge and felt it had to find it in order to be happy. The circle rolled around the countryside in search of its missing piece. Along the way it stopped to talk to the flowers and animals and warmed itself in sunshine.

Finally, the circle found its missing wedge and excitedly attached the piece to itself. Now the circle could be happy. It started to roll along so much faster that it didn't stop to talk to the friends it had made when it was incomplete. The circle grew unhappy being whole, removed the wedge and slowly rolled away.

How many times do we human beings say, "I would be happy if only I had...?" Yet we often find that life does not suddenly become perfect if we get that something. Each want is almost always immediately replaced by another.

True happiness is being grateful for what we have, as well as with what we haven't got.

Bless your Maker, who fills you with His good gifts. (Sirach 32:13)

Lord, in spite of my imperfections, remind me that I am made whole by Your love.

Can I Pray with Your Daughter?

Patheos blogger Rebecca Frech was loading groceries into her trunk while her 10-year-old daughter Ella, who is confined to a wheelchair, sat in the car. Frech then heard a woman nervously ask, "Excuse me, can I pray with your daughter?"

The woman identified herself as part of her church's ministry for the sick. She had seen Ella in the wheelchair and wanted to know if she could pray for her healing.

Frech looked at Ella, who gave her a sign that it was okay. "The stranger walked over to Ella," Frech wrote, "and repeated her question... When Ella nodded warily she asked, 'Is it okay if I hold your hands while I pray?' She held out her shaking hands, and, to my surprise, I watched my shy girl reach out in return."

On the ride home, Frech asked Ella what she thought about the stranger. Ella responded, "At first I thought it was weird, but then I thought 'This is what we're supposed to be doing, praying for people who need it.' You know, Mom?"

Frech realized that she and her daughter had experienced a moment of grace that day.

The prayer of faith will save the sick.
(James 5:15)

Grant me the courage to pray with the sick, Lord.

It's Not Over for You

After spending several years studying to be a screenwriter, Joan Bauer signed with a big talent agency in New York City. Two days later, she endured a debilitating car accident that left her in a great deal of pain and requiring neurosurgery.

Angry and scared, she imagined that she saw her dream of being a writer flying out a window. Then, she heard a voice inside of her giving her ideas for a story about a girl with a big dream. The voice said, "You can write this. It's not over for you."

Considering she had trouble even sitting at a desk, Bauer believed this to be impossible. But as she said during a *Christopher Closeup* interview, "Paragraph by paragraph, I wrote my first young adult novel and it ended up winning a big award." That novel was *Squashed* and it was the first of 12 novels geared toward young adults that Joan has now authored.

She concluded, "When we open ourselves up to that power that is beyond who we are and we let God have His way, let Him have our disappointments yet still believe that there's something good, that's what [life] has been for me again and again."

Cast your burdens on the Lord. (Psalm 55:22)

When disappointments crush me, Lord, guide me in a new direction.

Joy That Makes You Believe in Heaven

The sound of his eight-month-old daughter crying jolted Jake Frost out of a sound sleep in the middle of the night. He groggily made his way to her crib and brought her into the living room where he sat in a rocking chair to feed her. When the infant finished her bottle, she snuggled up against her father and returned to sleep.

Writing in *Catholic Digest*, Frost recalled, "I looked down at her lovely little face nestled in the crook of my arm. Her eyes closed, a smile dimpling her chubby apple-dumpling cheeks, an expression of contentment and serenity across her brow...It was beautiful. I was surprised by the moment of joy.

"It wasn't the frothy kind of jocularity that goes with party hats and off-key singing, but the quiet, seeping all the way down into your bones kind of joy that's almost too much to bear. The kind of joy that makes you believe in heaven... Maybe when we find ourselves ambushed unexpectedly by joy and beauty, it's because God has sent them out on a search-and-rescue mission to track us down and remind us that good things are still out there."

Let all who take refuge in You rejoice. (Psalm 5:11)

Sustain my spirit with moments of joy, Divine Savior.

A Nighttime Prayer

Lutheran pastor and German native Dietrich Bonhoeffer, who was imprisoned and killed for his anti-Nazi efforts during World War II, wrote a number of prayers over the course of his life. Here is one to be said at the end of the day:

"O Lord my God, thank You for bringing this day to a close; Thank You for giving me rest in body and soul. Your hand has been over me and has guarded and preserved me.

"Forgive my lack of faith and any wrong that I have done today, and help me to forgive all who have wronged me.

"Let me sleep in peace under Your protection, and keep me from all the temptations of darkness.

"Into Your hands I commend my loved ones and all who dwell in this house; I commend to You my body and soul. O God, Your holy name be praised. Amen."

When you lie down, your sleep will be sweet. Do not be afraid of sudden panic, or of the storm that strikes the wicked; for the Lord will be your confidence and will keep your foot from being caught. (Proverbs 3:24-26)

Grant me a peaceful and restful sleep, Lord, so that I can better serve You and my loved ones tomorrow.

A Rescue, Not a Recovery

Becca Winslow and Liz Wolthoff were roommates in northern New Jersey who also worked together. They were driving to work together one morning last winter when they suddenly found themselves airborne.

Swerving to avoid a tractor-trailer, their car hit a patch of ice, then a tightly-packed snowbank, launching them off a bridge on Route 80 and flying toward the Hackensack River, 60 feet below. Miraculously, a tree broke their fall as they headed toward the river. And more miraculously, they landed upright.

But they were badly hurt, with broken backs. Their heroes arrived within minutes—men from the Hackensack Fire Department, who expected to find bodies and instead found life. "It's a rescue," someone cried out, "not a recovery!"

After time in the hospital, the women had a chance to offer their thanks in person, at fire department headquarters. Gifts were exchanged, there was a speech by the mayor, and there were hugs and tears all around. "To know they'll have a chance at life and families," said one rescuer, "it feels really good."

Rescue me speedily. (Psalm 31:2)

Save us in times of peril, Gracious God, and bless the everyday heroes of our world.

Words That Work Wonders

May I? Thank you. Forgive me.

Three simple phrases, all familiar. Yet we don't hear them as often as we used to, and that's not as it should be. Pope Francis himself urged their frequent use.

Speaking at one of his general audiences last year, he said, "Sometimes it seems that we are becoming a civilization of bad manners and dirty words, as if they were a sign of emancipation. We hear them so often, even publicly. Kindness and an ability to say 'thank you' are almost seen as a sign of weakness."

Gratitude, the pope said, is at the heart of faith. "A Christian who does not know how to give thanks," he said, "is one who has forgotten God's language."

Family ties are at the heart of his thinking on this. The Holy Father said, "So many wounds in the family begin with the loss of those precious words, 'forgive me.'" Even when "plates fly" in the heat of the moment, apologies and forgiveness can work wonders, he concluded.

Be kind to one another...forgiving one another, as God in Christ has forgiven you. (Ephesians 4:32)

Messiah, may I choose my words wisely and humbly.

Simon Says Give

At age seven, Mandi Simon wanted to make life a little more enjoyable for children in need, so she came up with the idea to host birthday parties for them. With help from her mother, Dina, the Minnesota girl established the aptly named nonprofit Simon Says Give, which to date "has thrown birthday parties for 500 kids...who are growing up in poverty."

"I think it is really important for every kid to have one day, or at least a few hours, when it's all about them," the now 11-year-old Mandi told *Good News Network* writer Helaina Hovitz. "It's important for kids to go to a different environment and be able to have fun with their friends."

Recently, Mandi received the prestigious GlobeChanger Award, courtesy of the Jefferson Awards Foundation. The publicity from this honor garnered Simon Says Give worldwide acclaim, which Mandi hopes will only continue to grow. Her goal for the organization is to impact "two million kids by the year 2022." This just goes to show you're never too young (or too old) to make a difference.

Show yourself...a model of good works. (Titus 2:7)

Jesus, may we remember that actions speak louder than words.

Hope is Sweaty

When Father Jeff Putthoff arrived in Camden, New Jersey, in the late 1990s, he discovered that the high school graduation rate there was below 50 percent. That statistic didn't bode well for the city's younger generation. The Jesuit priest then turned this problem into an opportunity to serve his new community.

Father Putthoff founded Hopeworks 'N Camden, a nonprofit that teaches technology and entrepreneurial skills to teens and young adults. As reported by Jesuits.org, nearly 3,000 youths have earned the equivalent of a high school diploma from their in-house tutoring program.

Two hundred young people have gone on to college, while others have found jobs at companies like Google. "And about 30 percent of Hopeworks' annual operating budget comes from businesses that students have created and run within the organization."

All that accomplishment took a lot of hard work combined with hope. But as Father Putthoff told the *Philly Voice,* "We're about claiming hope. Hope is sweaty. The people of Camden taught me that."

My hope is from Him. (Psalm 62:5)

Inspire me to do the hard work that hope requires, Lord.

The $10,000 Thank You

In January of 2015, Marilyn Mecham got a call from Kevin Perz, a former student in her cooking class at Parkway Central High School in Chesterfield, Missouri. Perz graduated in 1977 and just wanted to express his appreciation to her for being such a great teacher. Two days later, Mecham received a handwritten note from him in the mail with a check for $10,000.

Perz had done this sort of thing before. In 1992, he sent $5,000 to his calculus teacher, and two decades later, he sent $10,000 to his business teacher. "Everybody can always think back to someone in their life who had an impact," Perz told *ABC News,* "if it's a teacher or a Boy Scout leader or anyone."

In his note, Perz wrote, "The enclosed Christmas gift is intended to be 100% used on you and your personal life."

Mecham cried over the gratitude shown to her and shared her thoughts on Facebook. "Gratitude is something in this society today that we just don't do enough of," she said. "It's made me stop and think: Who do I want to thank?"

You will be enriched in every way for your great generosity. (2 Corinthians 9:11)

Lord, may we strive to live in a state of perfect gratitude.

The Friendship Nine

The crime was clear-cut, and it turned out to be punishable by working on a chain gang for one month. What did the nine men do to bring on such a penalty? They were all black, and they had the effrontery to sit down at an all-white lunch counter, that's what.

That all took place 55 years ago, at a McCrory's 5 & 10 in Rock Hill, South Carolina, and it stood on the books for all that time. But finally last year the eight surviving members of the "Friendship Nine"—all students at Friendship Junior College—heard a judge wipe the slate clean.

"We cannot rewrite history," said Judge Mark Hayes last January, "but we can right history." He signed an order vacating the men's convictions. Spectators cheered, and one member of the group, Clarence Graham, spoke for them all when he said:

"It's been a long wait. We are sure now that we made the right decision for the right reason. Being nonviolent was the best thing that we could have done."

His soul hates the lover of violence.
(Psalm 11:5)

Guide me in creating change in this world through peaceable means, Prince of Peace.

I Wish You Could See What I See

Ellen Stumbo acknowledges that life with her special-needs daughters can sometimes be difficult. They deal with Down Syndrome, cerebral palsy, poor speech, and more. But their life together can also be glorious, which is a message she shared on her blog recently. Here are some excerpts:

"My kids are so much more than what your eyes perceive...I wish you could see how typical our lives are. Sibling fights, trips to the park, grilling burgers in the backyard...I wish you could recognize the sweet sound of those labored words, and how hearing, 'I love you' even with missing sounds, is beautiful. I wish you could see that we love our life, and we love our family, and we love how well we fit together, all of us flawed in our own way, all of us loved for exactly who we are.

"Yes, I wish you could see the love. And I wish you could feel it too. Because it's the type of love that surprises you, because you never thought you could love this way. Love changes things, even perspectives. I know it changed mine."

Whoever becomes humble like this child is the greatest in the kingdom of heaven. (Matthew 18:4)

Messiah, remind us that love is the most powerful grace.

Everyone Wins with Finnegans

Let's hear it for Finnegans Beer! People in Minnesota can hardly be blamed for repeating the slogan, since all the profits from the beer that's sold—every penny of it—goes to feed the hungry. That's a great record, and Finnegans means to make sure it keeps going for a long time to come.

Here's the way the arrangement works: all the profits from the beer sold to restaurants, bars and liquor stores go into the Finnegans Community Fund, which in turn buys produce from local farms and donates it to food banks in the area. Since the firm was founded in 2000, it's donated more than half a million dollars to the anti-hunger campaign.

Jessica Trygstad wrote about the company in *The Catholic Spirit,* newspaper of the St. Paul-Minneapolis Archdiocese, pointing out that next to Newman's Own brand, Finnegans is the second longest-running company in the U.S. with a 100 percent profit business model.

"The most important thing for me," said Jacquie Berglund, Finnegans' founder, "is creating wealth—and then giving it back."

It is better to give alms than to lay up gold. (Tobit 12:8)

Inspire businesses to help the less fortunate, Jesus.

An Angelic Meteorologist?

Nick Gregory, the chief meteorologist for Channel 5 in New York, has a second passion as well: he's a licensed pilot. And if more than a few people qualify as licensed pilots these days, Gregory has yet another calling that might pique your interest. He's a member of Angel Flight, an organization which provides flights for people with medical needs (or their families) to destinations they couldn't otherwise afford. The pilots are volunteers—as is Gregory, a member of the Angel Flight board.

David Hinckley, the *Daily News* TV critic, wrote about Gregory's avocation, pointing out that Angel Flight doesn't provide emergency medical transport. Rather it serves long-term patients who need treatment far from home. That would include one little girl that Gregory particularly remembers, a child with brittle bone disease he's taken from Pennsylvania to Montreal several times.

"The last time she was maybe five," Gregory recalls. "She had a walker, but she could get herself on and off the plane. She was so proud of that and gave me a big hug. It's a good feeling!"

By such work we must support the weak. (Acts 20:35)

Lord, inspire me to be an angel to someone in need.

From the Crack House to West Point

When Leah Chavez discovered she was pregnant, abortion or adoption were the only two options she was given by her family. When she refused both, she was thrown out of her home. After giving birth to her son, Dion, the hardships continued.

As reported by Wayne Coffey in New York's *Daily News,* Chavez "wound up living with her baby in a crack house and other sorry outposts in the poorest precincts in Phoenix. She wound up being forced into prostitution, getting by with food stamps and public assistance." Through it all, she remained devoted to giving her son the best life possible.

Twenty-two years later, Dion graduated from West Point as an accomplished swimmer "with an economics degree and a commission as a first lieutenant." He told Coffey, "My mother dropped everything to support me. She was the one to teach me that if you want something you have to be the one to make it happen. I wake up every morning with the intent to work towards achieving my goals because I know it will reinforce the fact that my mother was the best mother I could have ever asked for."

Since my mother bore me You have been my God. (Psalm 22:10)

Guide all mothers to choose life, Creator.

A Lesson in Accountability

After former Boston Red Sox pitcher Curt Schilling posted a congratulatory message to his daughter on Twitter for making it onto the Salve Regina University softball team, he was met with a string of sexually vulgar responses about her from young men thinking they were making anonymous comments.

Despite having worked in baseball locker rooms for his entire career, Schilling was shocked at the level of depravity he encountered in the comments that demeaned and debased his daughter. So, he decided to do something about it.

It turns out the anonymous commenters weren't as anonymous as they thought. Schilling tracked down their identities and publicly reprimanded them on his blog. One young man got fired from his job as a result; the other was suspended from school.

Schilling was happy to give these young adults a lesson in accountability, and hopes that others will learn from their mistakes.

On the day of judgment you will have to give an account for every careless word you utter. (Matthew 12:36)

May my words always respect the dignity of others, Savior.

Forgive the Weather Forecasters

In late January 2015, weather forecasters predicted that a paralyzing blizzard would hit the New York/New Jersey area. Major roadways as well as public transportation were closed down as a result.

The snowstorm, however, wasn't as bad as expected. The three feet of anticipated snow turned out to be only one foot. While most people were grateful to be spared, there were others who complained that the meteorologists had gotten it so wrong.

Well, here's some perspective. Meteorology is a science, but not always an exact one. Weather patterns can change quickly and deviate from the path they were supposed to follow. It's better to be over-prepared than under-prepared.

And here's another scenario to consider. Let's say you were in a car accident. Your vehicle sustained minor damage, but you escaped unscathed. Would you complain, "Darn it, that wasn't as bad as I expected!"—or would you say, "Thank God, it wasn't that bad." Chances are you'd pick the latter, so if the weather this winter isn't as bad as expected, be grateful.

An intelligent person will not complain. (Sirach 10:25)

Help me maintain a positive outlook, Lord.

The Purge

Matt Archbold asked his five kids to clean the front room of their house because "it looked like a tornado teamed up with a rabid chimpanzee in a toy factory." Reluctantly, the kids did as he asked, but then his wife made the task even more of a challenge. She told them they needed to give away some of the old toys they no longer played with.

Heartbroken at having to give away their old memories, they complied anyway. But then Mrs. Archbold made a final request: pick a few more toys to give away to poor children.

Archbold saw rebellion in his children's eyes until his wife dropped a loaded question on them. "Doesn't Jesus want you to share?" she asked. Writing in *Catholic Digest,* Archbold recalled, "This disconcerted them. They looked around at each other, unsure. They were all set to go up against their mother, but not Jesus. It was a clever strategy, I'll admit. If you're going to tag team, having Jesus on your side is a pretty good partner."

And so, the Archbold kids once again complied. But that day in their home will forever be known as "The Purge."

Share what you have. (Hebrews 13:16)

Help me appreciate the humor of family life, Jesus.

Here's to Somebody

Here's a story you may have heard before. It's about four people named Everybody, Somebody, Anybody, and Nobody.

There was an important job to do in the organization to which they all belonged. Everybody was asked to do it. Everybody was sure that Somebody would do it.

In reality, Anybody could have done it. But Nobody did it. Somebody got angry about that because it was Everybody's job.

Nobody realized that Everybody wouldn't do it. It ended up with Everybody blaming Somebody. That meant that Nobody could really blame Anybody.

Sound familiar? You can give it a different ending. All you have to do is decide that you want to be Somebody. If you do not do your job, who will?

The people did the work faithfully.
(2 Chronicles 34:12)

Carpenter from Nazareth, help me to work with care and diligence, giving all praise to You.

The Kindness Diaries, Part One

Leon Logothetis originally moved to the United States from England where he worked as a successful broker. Despite earning excellent money, he felt miserable and, at times, suicidal until he abandoned his comfortable life to walk across America with only $5 in his pocket. That journey became the basis for a book and television show, during which Logothetis encountered a lot of good people who showed him kindness.

When he returned to Los Angeles, he still believed he wasn't living the life he really wanted to pursue. Then he saw a homeless man holding a sign that read, "Kindness is the best medicine," and it triggered a new goal.

Logothetis decided to travel around the world and literally live off the kindness of strangers. He wouldn't spend any money on food, gas, or shelter himself. Everything would have to be provided by the people he met along the way. In turn, he would respond to people's generosity with kindnesses of his own—and chronicle his adventures in a book called *The Kindness Diaries*.

So what happened? More of the story tomorrow.

**Kindness is like a garden of blessings.
(Sirach 40:17)**

May kindness become second nature to me, Divine Savior.

The Kindness Diaries, Part Two

During his travels, Leon Logothetis met Willy, a man from Scotland who had moved to Colorado and dedicated his life to helping others after hearing Billy Graham speak in 1984. He and his wife Cheri were working at a retirement home where they planned to celebrate the 96th birthday of a resident named Kay.

In *The Kindness Diaries*, Logothetis quotes Willy as saying, "If we don't bring [Kay] cake, no one else will." When Logothetis met Kay, she said, "[Willy] makes me feel like I'm part of the human race and not just some old leftover luggage."

Logothetis realized that this was the perfect opportunity to show kindness to a man who was helping others. When he discovered that Willy and Cheri were going to miss their son's wedding in Scotland because they couldn't afford the plane fare, he paid for their trip himself. Willy shed tears of gratitude.

Regarding Willy, Logothetis recalled, "We turn on the news and it's all bad. Willy was someone who showed me how much goodness there really is out there."

More kindnesses tomorrow.

Let us work for the good of all. (Galatians 6:10)

Remind us to care for lonely seniors, Divine Savior.

The Kindness Diaries, Part Three

Another example of selfless goodness that Leon Logothetis encountered came on the streets of Pittsburgh. He approached a man in a park, told him what he was doing, and asked if he could provide him with a place to stay. The man, named Tony, said that he was homeless and living on the streets.

At first, Logothetis was ashamed at having imposed upon someone in such a dire situation. But as he explained during a *Christopher Closeup* interview about his book *The Kindness Diaries,* "[Tony] offered to put me up for the night, which was basically to sleep next to him. He protected me, he fed me, he gave me some of his clothes. I was sleeping on the streets next to this man who had nothing, and gave me everything!

"The next morning, I felt that I needed to help this man, so I set him up in an apartment and sent him back to school because he wanted to become a chef...Tony says to me, 'Leon, you changed my life.' But what he doesn't realize is that he changed my life. Tony changed my life."

Tomorrow, Logothetis sums up his travels.

Let us love...in truth and action. (1 John 3:18)

May we learn from those who have little but give much, Messiah.

The Kindness Diaries, Part Four

The Kindness Diaries is filled with Leon Logothetis's adventures in the United States, Europe, India, Cambodia, Vietnam, and Canada, but things don't always go his way—at least not initially. He admits that pain and struggle and asking people for help are humbling experiences.

However, he engaged in this "social experiment to take myself out of my comfort zone and to connect myself with the rest of humanity. The magic is the power of human connection."

Logothetis also hopes that readers take another lesson from his book: "Kindness doesn't have to be a grand expedition, like traveling around the world. That's just one form of kindness. Kindness can simply be saying, 'Have a happy day!' to a barista at Starbucks. It's a spectrum. You have the small acts and you have the big acts. But it's a way of life. It's a smile when you check into a hotel, it's a 'good day' to someone you see on the street. Little things like that go a long way."

> **The fruit of the Spirit is love, joy, peace, patience, kindness, generosity, faithfulness. (Galatians 5:22)**

Guide me in making more human connections grounded in kindness, Father.

Kids Kicking Cancer

Rabbi Elimelech Goldberg believes in putting faith over fear. The former director of Camp Simcha for children battling cancer once taught a five-year-old boy a breathing technique to help him through a tough chemotherapy session. He was pleased to see the boy barely noticed when the needle was removed.

This gave Rabbi Goldberg a brilliant idea: why not start a nonprofit for children with life-threatening illnesses? Since he is a black belt in Choi Kwang-Do, this charity would offer free karate lessons, so that these youngsters could literally fight the physical and emotional pain that come with their diagnoses.

To date, Kids Kicking Cancer has aided over 5,000 children worldwide. The mission is a personal one, too. Rabbi Goldberg lost his two-year-old daughter, Sara, to cancer over 40 years ago. "When children get a diagnosis like cancer or any other major disease, they lose all sense of feeling that they're controlling their lives," he told *CNN*. "We teach kids how to control their pain and make them feel powerful...[We] give children the tools to find the light that was already theirs."

The Lord is my light...whom shall I fear? (Psalm 27:1)

God, grant me the courage to face my fears.

The Courage of Her Convictions

The Civil Rights movement owes much to the courage of one woman: Rosa Parks. In 1955, she refused to give up her seat on the bus to a white man. The event sparked protests and boycotts which led to the Supreme Court ruling that racial segregation is unconstitutional.

"I have learned over the years that knowing what must be done does away with fear," she said later.

"When I sat down on the bus that day, I had no idea history was being made—I was only thinking of getting home. But I had made up my mind...I did not feel any fear sitting there. I felt the Lord would give me the strength to endure whatever I had to face. It was time for someone to stand up—or in my case, sit down. So I refused to move."

Let God guide you in living a life filled with courage.

I am continually with You; You hold my right hand. You guide me with Your counsel, and afterward You will receive me with honor. (Psalm 73:23-24)

Father, strengthen me to perform selfless acts of courage.

A 99-Year-Old's Labor of Love

Sometimes the world can treat senior citizens as if they have nothing left to contribute to society. Ninety-nine-year-old Lillian Weber proves that theory wrong.

In 2011, Weber, of Scott County, Iowa, saw a documentary about a charity called Little Dresses for Africa. The organization's website explains that they distribute hand-sewn dresses "to orphanages, churches and schools in Africa to plant in the hearts of little girls that they are worthy!" Over two million dresses have been handed out so far.

Weber, who's been sewing since age eight, told the *Quad-City Times* that she "thought it would be a great idea...to help some people who live far away." She makes a new dress every day because it gives her purpose and she likes to keep busy. She's already sewn 900 dresses and hopes to hit the 1,000 mark by the time she reaches her 100th birthday.

That doesn't mean she's going to put down her sewing needles, though. "When I get to that thousand, if I'm able to, I won't quit," she told *WQAD-TV*. "I'll go at it again."

Do not cast me off in the time of old age. (Psalm 71:9)

Divine Creator, use me to fulfill some higher purpose.

Spiritually Able

David and Mercedes Rizzo didn't know how they would raise their autistic daughter Danielle in the Catholic faith because they couldn't find any material to help them. So, they paved new ground themselves and are sharing what they learned in the book *Spiritually Able: A Parent's Guide to Teaching the Faith to Children with Special Needs.*

During a *Christopher Closeup* interview, the Rizzos admitted that the odds sometimes seemed "insurmountable," but their parish church was "very welcoming and willing to help us."

When asked what priests and parishioners can do to enhance that spirit of welcome, David said, "[We] want them to know that we're not being bad parents when our children [misbehave] or make noise or don't seem focused. That's part of the disability; it's not a sign of their irreverence. That gives us the opportunity for the child to learn the expected behaviors. And they will, because children with disabilities *do* learn. It is possible for them to learn to attend Mass, participate, and become an active participant in the faith."

Let the little children come to Me. (Mark 10:14)

Help me be welcoming to special needs children and their families, Jesus.

They Welcomed Everyone

In the 1840s and 50s, want ads still ran in New York newspapers stating, "Neither Irish nor Catholic need apply." Members of the anti-Catholic Know-Nothing party were elected to office throughout the country, and there were anti-Catholic riots in Brooklyn. So how did Catholics finally become accepted in the land to which they'd fled to find religious freedom?

During a *Christopher Closeup* interview, Pat McNamara, author of *New York Catholics,* explained, "The Catholics just wore them down. They kept coming and building churches and schools...and the hospital system and old age homes...and they started these orphanages, where they welcomed children of all denominations or none, of all races, of all backgrounds...

"One of the great pioneers of Catholic childcare was a priest named John Drumgoole, who said, 'I'll take any kid from any religion, background, race; I don't care.' And he did. He created Mount Loretto in Staten Island, which at the time was the largest childcare institution in the United States."

There is no longer Jew or Greek...for all of you are one in Christ Jesus. (Galatians 3:28)

Guide us in bridging divisions by welcoming strangers, Holy Spirit.

Call Your Parents

At the 2015 Academy Awards ceremony, actor J.K. Simmons earned the Oscar for Best Supporting Actor. His acceptance speech could have won him another award: Best Son.

Simmons appropriately started off by thanking his wife and children for their support of him and his career. Then, he encouraged the crowd with an important message.

He said, "Call your mom. Everybody, call your dad...If you're lucky to have a parent or two alive on this planet, call them. Don't text. Don't email. Call them on the phone, tell them you love them and thank them and listen to them for as long as they want to talk to you." He concluded his speech by saying, "Thank you, Mom and Dad."

It was refreshing to see an actor on one of the most-watched broadcasts of the year celebrate not himself, but the mother and father whose love and sacrifices shaped him as a person. It was also a reminder for millions of viewers—and each of us—to do the same.

So what are you waiting for? Go call your mom or dad.

The glory of children is their parents. (Proverbs 17:6)

Inspire children to better appreciate their parents, Father.

Pulling People Out of Their Own Pain

Volunteering to help others doesn't just have a benefit for them; it has a positive effect on you as well.

Peter J. Economou is a cognitive and behavioral psychologist in Bloomfield, New Jersey, who notes the health benefits of volunteering. While it's good for people of all ages, he told *Costco Connection* magazine's Malia Jacobson that it's especially "beneficial to adults over 65, or individuals with health woes." The reason? "My theory is that it pulls people out of their own pain."

Jacobson adds, "Those experiencing symptoms of disease or illness also can experience significant gains; research shows that patients with chronic pain have lower levels of depression and fewer painful symptoms while volunteering."

If you're dealing with illness but are still able to reach out to others in some way with your time or talent, consider opportunities to do so in your community or church. It could be an effective painkiller with no side effects.

We are what He has made us, created in Christ Jesus for good works. (Ephesians 2:10)

In bringing healing to others, may I find it myself, Lord.

Brake that Fall into Anger

The elevator is not a modern invention. Lifts have been used in construction from the time the pyramids were built. But they were too dangerous for passengers. Cables could break with disastrous results.

Then, in 1854, Elisha Otis of Vermont found a way to make elevators safe. His invention used a large compressed spring. If the elevator cable went slack, this spring automatically snapped out, pushing two iron bars into notched guide rails in the elevator shaft. This locked the elevator in place, protecting passengers.

When tempers snap and anger gets out of control, the results can also be disastrous. Obviously, we can't help feeling angry at times because anger is a normal emotion. But we can put a "safety lock" on what we say or do.

Then, while keeping our anger in check, we can explore the cause of the anger and see what can be done about it without going off the rails.

Refrain from anger, and forsake wrath. Do not fret — it leads only to evil. (Psalm 37:8)

Help us keep our anger in check, patient Jesus who knew anger, but so often checked it.

The Homeless Guardian Angel

When six-year-old Sergio Zepeda wandered off from his San Jose, California home, his parents weren't just panicked because of his age; they feared for his life because he has autism and has trouble communicating.

KTVU-TV reported that the boy was missing for 17 hours before police finally found him in an unusual place: a homeless encampment near a local highway.

A resident of the camp, Jose Salmeron, had found Sergio wandering through the area and offered him food, water and a blanket. Meanwhile, another homeless person at the camp called 911.

According to the *San Jose Mercury News*, Salmeron said, "We're not heroes. It was the only right thing to do. When you see a helpless kid like that, you are supposed to do the right thing and just call the cops right away."

Remember, guardian angels come in various forms.

Whoever welcomes one such child in My name welcomes Me, and whoever welcomes Me welcomes not Me but the one who sent Me. (Mark 9:37)

Guide the lost and suffering, Jesus, to peace and security with You.

A Lit Candle, An Act of Hope

Father Ron Rolheiser, OMI, once shared the following reflection on the power of lighting a candle: "In the days of apartheid in South Africa, Christians there used to light candles and place them in windows as a sign to themselves and to others that they believed that some day this injustice would end.

"A candle burning in a window was a sign of hope and a political statement. The government didn't miss the message. It passed a law making it illegal to place a lit candle in a window, the offense being equal to owning a firearm, both considered equally dangerous.

"Lit candles, more than firearms, overthrew apartheid. Hope, not guns, is what ultimately transforms things. To light a candle as an act of hope is to say to yourself and others that, despite anything that might be happening in the world, you are still nursing a vision of peace and unity based upon something beyond the present state of things. And this hope is based upon deeper realities and powers than the world admits."

You are the God of the lowly...protector of the forsaken, savior of those without hope. (Judith 9:11)

Help me to choose hope every day, King of Kings.

Ashes and the Human Condition

There is something inside us that makes us yearn for some supernatural assurance in our physical world. We still use the ordinary things in our lives to indicate and remind us of hidden mysteries.

That is why Ash Wednesday continues to mean something special. At the beginning of Lent, we are marked with ashes as a reminder of our union with Jesus and His Passion. They also speak of our need to do penance, to prepare ourselves for the central mystery of our faith.

Annually, we are brought back to our relationship with God—Father, Son and Holy Spirit. It highlights our human condition.

We are marked as people who try to be better, to be good, to be more than we thought we were capable of being. And always, we are reminded of our mortality and of God's plan for our eternity.

Give them a garland instead of ashes, the oil of gladness instead of mourning. (Isaiah 61:3)

Mark me as Yours, O Lord, and forgive my failings.

Lent Leads to Human Connections

In 2014, Kerry Weber, the Christopher Award-winning author of *Mercy in the City*, shared her thoughts on Lent with Catholic Relief Services. She said:

"It's sometimes easy to think that Lent is all about us [and] what am I giving up for Lent...While Lent is a time of personal spiritual growth, we have to remember also that it's more than just the Catholic version of some self-help program...

"The season of Lent is a little like riding a bus...It's tempting to put on our headphones, hunker down into our seats, ignore everybody else, and keep to ourselves. Something is lost when we do that. We lose that chance for connection...

"The 40 days of Lent give us time...to pray and fast and give alms, not to just check these things off our Lenten to-do list, but to be more conscious of the people around us...We really are on this ride together. Your Lenten journey and my Lenten journey are intertwined in the messiness of our everyday lives. So this Lent, I challenge you to reach out, to acknowledge the dignity of the people around you, and to enjoy the ride."

**All of you are one in Christ Jesus.
(Galatians 3:28)**

Deepen my bonds with You and others this Lent, Father.

A Giant's Heart

Last Valentine's Day, Steve Weatherford dressed up as Cupid. He wore a white tunic, and on his back were strapped a pair of tiny red wings. He held a little bow and arrow in his hands. What's wrong with this picture? Plenty, as it turns out.

Steve Weatherford is a grown man, and what's more he's a punter for the New York Football Giants. But there's also plenty right with the picture, as Ebenezer Samuel pointed out in his report on the incident for New York's *Daily News*. The scene took place at New York's Hospital for Special Surgery, and Weatherford was there to visit sick children—as he often does.

"It's not uncommon for NFL players to get involved in charitable efforts," said Samuel in his story, "but few are more involved in the community than Weatherford."

The punter explained: "These kids, they're going through things that a lot of them don't deserve to go through. For me to come out here and spend 45 minutes...It's a small investment of time for me, but they'll remember it forever."

The integrity of the upright guides them. (Proverbs 11:3)

Help me bring small joys to others, Father.

What Makes a Great Dad?

Verily magazine's Nell O'Leary has been happily married for five years and now has three children. She realizes that when young women are dating, they might not wonder what kind of father their boyfriend will be someday, but she thinks they should. And she offers several qualities for them to look out for:

- **He listens.** "When something is really on your heart, does he set aside his own thoughts...and tune in to just you? Good dads are great listeners."

- **He is patient.** "How is your boyfriend's patience in general?...Good dads are profoundly patient: first in welcoming the child, and later in coping with the lack of sleep, free time, and autonomy that parenthood brings."

- **He is sacrificial.** "Good dads are ready to sacrifice...If he's not ready to sacrifice when you are dating, it's unlikely the pattern will change when the ante is upped."

- **He has a sense of humor.** "The man who can laugh at himself has the best sense of humor in life. Good dads appreciate life—and that's a sense of humor in itself."

Let love be genuine. (Romans 12:9)

Guide those looking for a spouse to choose wisely, Lord.

Papa Giovanni's Relationship Advice

It's unlikely that many romances have started near the glass sarcophagus of St. Pius X's remains in St. Peter's Basilica, but that's where Luigi and Fernanda Bistacco's 55-year relationship began in 1960. The 18-year-old Fernanda, from New Jersey, was kneeling there in prayer when Luigi, a Vatican gendarme (guard), initiated a conversation and offered to show the teen and her mother around Rome. They agreed and spent several days together, during which Luigi and Francesca fell in love and got engaged.

She would return to Rome in three years for the wedding and to live there. But as the wedding date neared, Fernanda's mother put the kibosh on her move. If Luigi wanted to marry her, he would have to come to America.

Recalling their story in *New Jersey Catholic* magazine, Luigi said he consulted with Papa Giovanni (a.k.a Pope John XXIII) about what to do. The pontiff told him, "Follow your heart." Luigi did. The couple's civil marriage took place in Rome while the church wedding happened in New Jersey. When they visited the pope's summer residence, he blessed Francesca and told her, "You will be happy." His prediction was correct.

Rejoice in the wife of your youth. (Proverbs 5:18)

May the love of married couples endure, Lord.

Enduring Criticism

Criticism. It's a word with a lot of negative connotations. Listening to criticism and putting it into perspective is hard for most of us.

Here's a quote that just might help you: "I do the very best I can, I mean to keep going. If the end brings me out all right, then what is said against me won't matter. If I'm wrong, ten angels swearing I was right won't make a difference."

That piece of wisdom was framed on the office wall of British statesman Winston Churchill. The words were said by President Abraham Lincoln.

Somehow it seems fitting that a leader who guided his bitterly divided country through the turmoil of a civil war could inspire another leader through the bleak days of a world war.

Follow their example. Do your best. That's all anyone can ask of you. Even yourself.

If the humble person slips, they even criticize him; he talks sense, but is not given a hearing. (Sirach 13:22)

When subject to criticism, Lord, remind me of Lincoln's example of courage and wisdom.

Moving Through the Midwinter Blues

Cold weather, snow, and ice can sometimes lead us to experience the midwinter blues. Despite the season's trials, however, Cincinnati-based writer Matt Litton shared his reasons for embracing winter on BustedHalo.com:

- "Nothing reminds me of my childhood like peering through a frosted window in the early morning hours to discover a pristine coat of snow unmarred by footprints or tire tracks…Winter can help us remember that we are at our best when we approach the world with a childlike faith and wonder."

- "While the earth is nestled under white blankets, all is still, and we should value these moments to listen and to rest because we know that God ultimately resides in stillness."

- "We endure winter's long residency precisely because the coming warmth of new life is inevitable. Winter teaches us that spring eventually arrives in its own time and there is nothing we can do about it except walk willingly in the cold and allow it to run its course."

Bless the Lord, winter cold and summer heat; sing praise to Him. (Daniel 3:67)

Teach me to appreciate every season of life, Lord.

An Overlooked Trait in a Spouse

Kevin A. Thompson, pastor of Christ Community Church in Fort Smith, Arkansas, knows that young people hoping to get married often look for qualities like a good sense of humor or common interests in a spouse. But he advises considering a different characteristic: "Find someone who suffers well."

Pastor Thompson wrote on his blog, "The older a person gets, the more we realize that suffering is not a rare occurrence, but is a common aspect of our lives...Some live in denial—unable to confront the deep realities of life. Some live in despair—unable to recognize the convergence of laughter and tears...

"Yet, when our spouse knows how to suffer, when they don't live in denial, but confront the sorrows of life; when they don't live in despair but know how to laugh and cry at the same time; when they offer support and hope in all of life's challenges; when they can see the big picture of life, every sorrow is matched with love and every hurt paired with healing."

We are afflicted in every way, but not crushed. (2 Corinthians 4:8)

May husbands and wives be a comfort to each other during sickness and health, Father.

Humble Heroes Save a Life

Four New York City transit workers were honored last year for saving the life of a fellow employee.

The chairman of the Metropolitan Transportation Authority, Thomas Prendergast, presented "Hometown Hero" awards to track workers Clyde Ferguson, Louis Albino, Stewart Azzato and David Soto for coming to the rescue of Hoi-Shan Leung, who was in danger of falling 60 feet—and, in all probability, to his death.

Leung had tripped during a track replacement job and was knocked unconscious. New York's *Daily News*, which was a partner in this third annual award ceremony, reported on the men's story.

"They saved my life," said Leung. "It's good to be alive. I'm alive because of them."

Albino, speaking for his co-rescuers, shrugged off all references to the heroics they had demonstrated. "I was just helping my buddy," he said. "This is just great. He was able to see his granddaughter's first birthday. That's awesome!"

[We] cry to You in our distress, and You will hear and save. (2 Chronicles 20:9)

Imbue me with courage in all aspects of my life, Lord.

When God Hits You Over the Head

PJ Anderson worked as a youth minister in Chicago for several years while performing music on the side. When doors started closing in his ministry work, he felt betrayed by God and wondered why He would allow these things to happen.

That period led Anderson to move to Nashville to pursue a full-time music career—and it also taught him to move through dark times in a positive way. During a *Christopher Closeup* interview about his album *Rise*, he said, "There are times when you [think], 'I'm praying and trying to do things for You, God, but I don't know what You're doing for me.' That's when the red flag needs to go up. It's not about what God's doing for us; it's about what we continue to give every day and how we allow Him to work through us. And He is.

"God is working through us and giving us grace...It took God hitting me over the head to realize that doors were closing in youth ministry [because] He wanted me to do something different, and that was writing [and playing] music for Him."

**He will make straight your paths.
(Proverbs 3:6)**

When I have difficulty seeing Your plan for my life, Lord, strengthen my trust in You.

The Way of Serenity, Part One

A stranger stopped Father Jonathan Morris on the street one day because he recognized him from TV. "I want you to know I don't believe in God, but I'm still trying to be a good person," said the stranger. Father Jonathan engaged the man in friendly conversation, before giving his usual parting words: "Would you say a prayer for me and I'll say a prayer for you?"

As soon as he said it, he laughed at his mistake and added, "Well, I'll say a prayer for you." The man smiled and walked away, but then turned back to say, "I don't believe in prayer, because I don't know if anyone is listening, but I do like that Serenity Prayer."

That response was an eye-opener for Father Jonathan. He knew the Serenity Prayer: "Lord, grant me the serenity to accept the things I cannot change, courage to change the things I can, and wisdom to know the difference." Now, he wondered, "Why [does] this gentleman who doesn't believe in God recognize the goodness or truth or beauty of this prayer?"

More of the story tomorrow.

Let them seek peace and pursue it.
(1 Peter 3:11)

Lead those who doubt You to experience the divine presence that exists within us all, Creator.

The Way of Serenity, Part Two

Following his encounter with the nonbeliever who appreciated the Serenity Prayer, Father Jonathan Morris realized that serenity is a common human longing in a world filled with violence, broken relationships, health problems, etc.

During an interview on *Christopher Closeup* about his book *The Way of Serenity*, Father Morris said that most people don't just want "the serenity of the one who puts everything aside and says, 'I'm not gonna pay attention to this bad world. I'm gonna live in my own little world.' It's a serenity that's much deeper than that. In the midst of difficulties, there's a peace of soul."

That peace of soul rests largely in our ability to follow the first piece of advice in the prayer: "What I think we're asking is, 'Lord, allow me to let go of the things that I should let go of.' That's hard to do. But deep down, we know that there are some things we need to let go of, feelings like anger and resentment."

Some concluding insights about serenity and humility tomorrow.

**Those who counsel peace have joy.
(Proverbs 12:20)**

Move me past anger towards true serenity, Divine Savior.

The Way of Serenity, Part Three

Serenity also involves being humble and not judging others. That lesson was brought home to Father Jonathan Morris when his parents visited him from Ohio. They were in Manhattan when his father spotted a shirtless, pony-tailed, gray-haired man wearing cowboy boots, jean shorts, and all sorts of chains around his neck. The elder Morris said, "Now I've seen it all."

The next day, said Father Morris, "I was in the church doing my morning prayer, and that same gentleman was over to the right praying on his knees in front of the Blessed Virgin Mary. I saw him as he was walking out of the church, and I said, 'Is there anything I can pray for you for?' He said, 'No, I do this every day. I just go and I thank God and the Mother of Jesus for all the blessings that they have allowed in my life.'"

Father Jonathan told his father what happened. It left him feeling humbled at having been wrongfully judgmental. Said Father Jonathan, "When you're grateful, you're humble, and the humble soul is the soul open to God and, essentially, peaceful."

God opposes the proud, but gives grace to the humble. (1 Peter 5:5)

Grant me the grace to be humble, Lord.

Finding Light in the Darkness

In February 2015, American humanitarian worker Kayla Mueller, who had been held hostage by the terrorist group ISIS, was confirmed as having been killed. Following her death, her last letter to her parents was released to the public, revealing how much she had relied on God throughout her ordeal. She wrote:

"I remember Mom always telling me that in the end, the only one you really have is God. I have come to a place in experience where, in every sense of the word, I have surrendered myself to our creator b/c literally there was no [one] else....By God + by your prayers I have felt tenderly cradled in freefall.

"I have been shown in darkness, light + have learned that even in prison, one can be free. I am grateful. I have come to see that there is good in every situation, sometimes we just have to look for it. I pray each day that if nothing else, you have felt a certain closeness + surrender to God as well + have formed a bond of love + support amongst one another."

If the earthly tent we live in is destroyed, we have a building from God...eternal in the heavens. (2 Corinthians 5:1)

Welcome my deceased loved ones into Your kingdom, Lord.

How Can I Care for the Sick?

Father Joe Krupp writes an advice column of sorts in *New Jersey Catholic* magazine, and recently received a question from a person who wanted to know how to minister to the sick in his parish. Father Joe's first suggestion was, "Pray for those who are sick and ask God to restore them. This binds us to their fate and allows the power of the Holy Spirit to unite us in God's heart and mind."

Next, he said, consider visiting the homebound and hospitalized. "Often, these folks could use a friend, and God may very well be calling you to be that friend. Bring over cards or checkers or a book. Bring pictures of your family and ask to hear about theirs." In addition, bring a parish bulletin and news of what's happening in the church so they still feel connected.

Finally, "See if your parish needs volunteers to take Communion to the homebound or those in the hospital. Ask to be trained and get on that list! You can and will find a special joy in bringing the presence of Christ through the gift of the Eucharist into the lives of those who are ill."

I will bind up the injured. (Ezekiel 34:16)

Christ, may we remember that even the smallest gesture can bring comfort and healing to the sick.

The Repentant Thief

About 12 years ago, the InterAsian Market and Deli in Nashville, Tennessee, was robbed at gunpoint. In September 2013, a man came into the deli and handed Somboon Wu, the owner's son, a note he insisted must be read. Although reluctant, Wu was astonished when he opened it. Inside the envelope was $400 and a handwritten letter that read exactly as follows:

"I am a drug addict. About 11 or 12 years ago I robber this store with a gun. I do not use drugs anymore and I feal I must make amends...I came in you're store...and I got a 6 pack of beer and ask for cigaretts, when the registar opened to give change I pulled out a gun and took about $300 from the register then drove away...I hope you will accept this money and find forgiveness. – Anonymous"

Wu told Nashville's *WSMV Channel 4,* "We get cynical, but this just slaps you in the face. There are good people out there, and they deserve a second chance...We just want to let him [the ex-drug addict] know...we forgive you."

Bear with one another...forgive each other. (Colossians 3:13)

Jesus, may we remember it is never too late for redemption.

Wired For Connections/Mentor Up!

Young people have learned a lot from the wisdom of their elders over the years, and no doubt they will continue to do so. But today, in terms of technology, the students have become the teachers. The organization Wired For Connections/Mentor Up is a perfect example of such a role reversal.

Founded two years ago by California teens Sean Butler and Carly Rudiger, this club matches up 15 high school students with an elderly man or woman. Once a week, usually on a Saturday, these youngsters from Carmel High School help their older companions navigate the daunting technological worlds of their laptops, smart phones, iPads, etc.

According to Butler, the volunteers benefit as much from these sessions as their pupils. "I can honestly say I've learned more during these sessions than I've taught," Rudiger recalled to Dennis Taylor of *truthAtlas*. "For me, just talking with them and learning their stories is what draws me back every time."

Like good stewards...serve one another with whatever gift each of you has received. (1 Peter 4:10)

God, may we learn to utilize our talents for the greater good.

Motivations for Meatless Fridays

If your idea of fasting during Lent means skipping meat on Fridays but splurging on seafood, you've missed something big. That's the word from none other than Pope Francis himself, who devoted one of his daily homilies last year to the subject.

A report in *Catholic News Service*, which covered the homily, pointed out that real fasting goes way beyond restricting your food choices for a day or so. It means cleansing your heart of all selfishness, and making room for those in need—in need of food or clothing, or of spiritual healing.

The pope asked that during Lent people think about what they can do for others who are in difficult situations—children and the elderly, for example.

"Love toward God and love to your neighbor are one," the pope said. "If you want to practice real penance, you have to do it before God and also with your brother and sister, your neighbor...What will you do for these people? What will your Lent be like?"

Give up your faults and direct your hands rightly, and cleanse your heart from all sin. (Sirach 38:10)

Turn my selfishness into selflessness, Holy Spirit.

A Happy (and Selfless) Anniversary

In his column for the *Catholic Standard,* Father William Byrne, pastor of St. Peter's Church in the nation's capital, took advantage of the 75th anniversary of the Washington, D.C. Archdiocese to list five ways to celebrate any major anniversary:

- **Pray.** "There's actually no better present."

- **The poor.** Father Byrne suggests giving to the poor as a way to help the celebration along. "The poor are the faces of Christ in our midst," he notes.

- **When giving, give wisely.** "The best way to give money to the poor is to give to those who know best how to use it. Catholic Charities knows their business."

- **Forgive.** Forgiveness might include our brother, sister, neighbor, cousin, boss, priest, friend. "The flow of love in our lives is the key to anniversary graces."

- **Yahoo!** "It is a sin not to enjoy the gifts that God gives us...God is amazingly generous and wants us to enjoy goodness and share it with others."

Let us celebrate the festival...with the unleavened bread of sincerity and truth. (1 Corinthians 5:8)

May I make You a part of every celebration, Father.

The Law of the Fallow Field

In his newsletter *Apple Seeds*, Father Brian Cavanaugh, TOR, shared a personal lesson he learned from living in rural Pennsylvania about the "Law of the Fallow Field." He wrote: "In farming there is a principle of crop rotation: a field is sectioned off by threes. In the first section, corn is grown; in the second section, potatoes or soybeans are planted; and the third section is left fallow, nothing is planted to give the soil a season of rest. In the following years, each section is rotated through the cycle.

"If you drive past a field with this type of planting, check out the section left fallow. Intentionally, nothing was planted in it. Yet you'll notice this section is filled with an abundance of weeds. Weeds—just like sin, vices, negative attitudes—[are] everywhere. You don't need to plant them; they just grow.

"However, to grow something positive like corn, potatoes, virtue, or teamwork, that has to be intentional, and you have to repeat it every growing season. Just because you grew something last year doesn't mean you can skip this year. Otherwise, those weeds/vices will sprout up in your fallow field."

**Sow for yourselves righteousness.
(Hosea 10:12)**

Help my virtues blossom, Jesus.

An Actor's Promise to God

Eduardo Verastegui had found success as an actor, model, and singer in his native Mexico, so he moved to Los Angeles in 2002 to pursue a career in Hollywood as well. That's when he realized how much media influences the way people think, and how the work he was choosing wasn't contributing anything positive to the world.

During a *Christopher Closeup* interview about his faith-based World War II movie *Little Boy,* he recalled, "[That changed after] a conversation I had with my English teacher. She asked me, 'Why are you an actor? How are you using your talent? Does every project you're involved with have the power to make a difference and elevate human dignity?' Little by little, she opened my eyes. One day, I made a promise to God and to my parents that I would never use my talents to do anything that would offend my faith, my family, and my Latino culture."

Verastegui wound up not working for four years. Ultimately, he started his own production company so he could create the types of films that he promised God he would make.

Fulfill what you vow. (Ecclesiastes 5:4)

May both my words and actions elevate human dignity, Creator.

The Work of His Hands

Here's some good advice from a second century bishop, Irenaeus of Lyon, about our relationship with our Creator:

"You are the work of God,
await the hand of the Artist
who does all things in due season.
Offer Him your heart, soft and
tractable and keep the form in
which the Artist has fashioned you.
Let the clay (of your being) be moist,
lest you grow hard
And lose the imprint of His fingers."

Centuries before Irenaeus, the prophet Jeremiah wrote that we are like clay in the potter's hand—God's hand. We need only be willing to be shaped by our Maker to fulfill His plans for us.

"Can I not do with you...as this potter has done?" says the Lord. "Just like the clay in the potter's hand, so you are in My hand." (Jeremiah 18:6)

Master Potter, form me, fashion me, into a fit vessel for Your Spirit.

A Family Doctor

The old-fashioned family doctor seems a quaint notion in these times of health plans and managed care. Dr. Matthew Warpick, one of the last of the breed, passed away at age 95—yet he served his patients right up until the end, seeing his last one the day before he died.

An urban version of the country doctor, Dr. Warpick worked six days a week from 6 a.m. to early afternoon in his Harlem, New York office. He often charged his mostly poor and working class clientele only what they thought they could pay.

Even though some considered the neighborhood dangerous, he stayed put. "I've got to take care of the people who have been loyal to me. I can't leave them alone," he said.

His patients taught him the values of honesty, good relations and loyalty, all of which meant more to him than money.

There may come a time when recovery lies in the hands of physicians, for they too pray to the Lord that He grant them success in diagnosis and in healing, for the sake of preserving life. (Sirach 38:13-14)

May I value human connections over money, Divine Giver.

Instruments of Joy

Joshua McLeod has been to poverty-stricken and war-torn countries around the world in his role as executive director of Watermelon Ministries, a Christian non-profit that uses media to spread the Gospel. It was a trip to an orphanage in Malawi, however, that left him overwhelmed with hopelessness. Then, an older boy entered the room and completely changed the mood.

The child was carrying a makeshift guitar made of a gas can and a block of wood. He started playing, and all the children's faces and attitudes became joyful. This set McLeod on a new mission. He founded an organization called Instruments of Joy.

The group's mission "is to equip orphans and aspiring musicians in the developing world with quality musical instruments in Jesus's name." New or used instruments are collected and given to volunteers making mission trips overseas to distribute.

McLeod said, "There are a lot of ways to fight poverty. We fight poverty by bringing beauty into areas of devastation and bringing joy through music."

Let us sing to the Lord. (Psalm 95:1)

Bring beauty and music to the world's dark places, Jesus.

The Name Game

Author Lisa Hendey sits in her usual pew whenever she attends Mass at her California church. She recognizes the other parishioners around her who have their favorite "pew spots" too. But Hendey recently realized that while she recognizes these people's faces, she doesn't know their names.

Writing on her Patheos blog, she noted, "We feel like 'family,' these pewmates and I. We're there together enough that I know when one couple's daughter is visiting or when a particular husband has to work the Sunday shift at his job. So does it matter if I don't know their names? Yes, I think it does."

Hendey believes that knowing people's names is a great way to build a spirit of community in her church—and she's determined to do a better job of it in the future.

Are there people you see all the time in church or elsewhere whose names you don't know? Consider introducing yourself. It could plant the seeds of a new friendship.

I was a stranger and you welcomed Me. (Matthew 25:35)

Getting to know new people can feel awkward, Father. Help me do it anyway.

Growing Up, Growing Good

Talk to a child about growing up and they probably think in terms of an age like 18 or 21—or an event like getting a driver's license or going off to college. But real maturity does not come so easily.

Saint Pope John XXIII offered some thoughts on growing up—within: "In a world of spiritual endeavor, as in the world of athletic competition, we must learn never to be content with the level we have reached but, with the help of God and with our own determined efforts, we must aim at ever greater heights, at continual improvement, so that we may in the end reach maturity, the measure of the stature of the fullness of Christ."

Complacency can interfere with the development of talent or ability. Certainly it can stunt a soul. Don't stop trying to be more than you are today. And grow well.

Go to the ant, you lazybones; consider its ways, and be wise...How long will you lie there, O lazybones? When will you rise from your sleep? (Proverbs 6:6,9)

Nourish me, Lord. Nurture me, so I may grow straight and true.

A Friend Indeed

Five boys from Franklin Elementary School in Mankato, Minnesota, already understand the idea of standing up for what's right. They proved their virtue by standing up for their special needs classmate, James Willmert.

This tightknit group resented the way Willmert was being teased, especially during recess. "They were using him [James] and taking advantage of him because he's easier to pick on, and that's just not right," Jack Pemble, one of the boys, told *KARE News*.

These five students—Pemble along with his buddies Jake, Landon, Gus and Tyler—started off their fifth grade school year by being a friend to Willmert, who needed some kindness. His learning disability makes no difference. To them, he is just James, their friend, an "awesome kid to hang out with" who loves sports and video games.

In recognition of their kindness to James, the five boys received the Spirit of Youth Award at the end of the school year. But to them, James's friendship is the greatest gift of all.

Two are better than one...One will lift up the other. (Ecclesiastes 4:12)

Father, may we always cherish the gift of true friendship.

Clean Cut, Clean Start

Nasir Sobhani was a drug addict, with a particular weakness for cocaine. Born in Japan, he later moved to Canada, where he underwent most of his rehab. "Luckily I had a home to always go to, my mum loved me too much to kick me out," the now sober 26-year-old told *Daily Mail Australia*. "I wasn't homeless, but...some of the people I was spending time with were...March 23rd, 2012...I became sober. Right after rehab, I decided I wanted to start cutting hair."

Sobhani soon obtained a job as a barber in Melbourne, Australia, where he moved shortly after his recovery. For over a year now, he has provided free haircuts to the homeless on his day off as part of his "Clean Cut, Clean Start" initiative.

Sobhani understands where these people are coming from, and how one kind gesture can make all the difference. In fact, he has been witness to many positive transformations in his clientele. "I love cutting hair," Sobhani concludes, "that service to humanity is service to God. I finally got my life back and I just want to give to others in the way that I know how to."

Like good stewards...serve one another.
(1 Peter 4:10)

Abba, move us past our mistakes to a clean start.

A Mid-Lent Review

How's your Lent going? If you find that you need to stay focused on your spiritual goals, here are five suggestions courtesy of columnist Mary DeTurris Poust—published in *Catholic New York*, newspaper of the New York Archdiocese:

- Don't bite off more than you can chew. Try to stretch beyond what you normally do, but don't aim for the impossible.

- If you're not spending time with God in prayer, you'll have a hard time getting out of the starting gate.

- Don't see backsliding as failure, but as an opportunity to figure out what your Lenten discipline should really be about.

- Don't use Lent as a way to achieve other goals. When Lent goes off course, it's because we want transformation on our own terms.

- When all else fails, just be kinder today than you were yesterday. If we can do that, even if we haven't followed through on our other plans, then we'll pass Lent with flying colors.

Is not this the fast that I choose...to share your bread with the hungry and bring the homeless poor into your house? (Isaiah 58:6-7)

May my heart grow closer to You this Lent, Jesus.

When Loyalty Trumps Dollars

They say that money talks, but apparently it's not loud enough for Alan Rosen to hear.

Rosen, owner of the Brooklyn, New York landmark Junior's restaurant, world-famous for its iconic cheesecake, turned down a cool $45 million from a developer who wanted to build a high-rise residential development on the restaurant's Flatbush Avenue site. The decision was made partly to ensure continued employment for the men and women who worked at Junior's, a point made by Rosen's father, Walter, 81.

"I felt bad for the help we've had for years," the elder Rosen said. "I really didn't want them to lose their jobs."

Alan Rosen said he weighed the future without the family business at its familiar location and couldn't go through with it. "Obviously it was not a financial decision," he said. "It was emotional."

His father approved. "You did the right thing," Walter Rosen said—and just about everyone in Brooklyn and beyond agreed.

Keep your lives free from the love of money. (Hebrews 13:5)

May we treasure people over profits, Divine Giver.

The Homer and the Handshake

When George Shuba of Youngstown, Ohio, died at 89 in September of 2014, he rated a long obituary in *The New York Times*. True, he had played baseball with the old Brooklyn Dodgers, but his career batting average was only .259 and he hit a grand total of just 24 home runs.

So what did he do that rated that big an obit in the *Times*? The headline says it all: "George Shuba Dies at 89: Offered Tolerant Gesture." That was it, but the gesture was important.

It happened in 1946, when Jackie Robinson made his debut with the Montreal Royals of the International League, the first black player in the history of organized baseball. He hit a homer that day, and when he'd run the bases George Shuba was there to greet him—with a warm handshake. Not many ballplayers were willing to shake the hand of a black man then, and it meant a lot.

A cameraman recorded the event, and Shuba, his son recalls, often used his copy to make a point. "I want you to remember what that stands for," he'd say. "You treat all people equally." End of lesson.

If you have come to me in friendship...my heart will be knit to you. (1 Chronicles 12:17)

Help me be a friend to the outcast, Lord.

Keeping Your Heart Healthy

Since heart disease is the leading killer of both men and women, *Verily* magazine's Kirsten Nunez offered several suggestions for keeping your heart healthy:

- **Know your genetics.** "The best baseline for cardiovascular disease (CVD) prevention is educating yourself on your family's history of heart health."

- **De-stress.** "With so much to do in so little time, relaxing can be hard. But slowing down will help your heart tremendously. Stress doesn't just lead to hypertension (abnormally high blood pressure) and insomnia. It also can trigger unhealthy behaviors, such as excessive drinking, smoking, and overeating."

- **Stay active.** "Exercise drastically decreases your risk by reducing hypertension and keeping your heart in tip-top shape." Dr. Martha Gulati of Ohio State University's Wexner Medical Center said, "The heart is a muscle and needs to be used. Exercise for 30 minutes daily, or even in three separate 10-minute intervals."

I pray that all may go well with you and that you may be in good health. (3 John 1:2)

Heal my heart both physically and spiritually, Creator.

Above and Beyond the Call of Duty

Off-duty Detective Patrick Blanc not only came through; he did so in the finest tradition of the New York Police Department. And he did so in the midst of tragedy, adding luster to the feat.

Detective Blanc came across a house fire in the St. Albans neighborhood of Queens, New York, in time to see the bodies of brothers John, 11, and Andrew, 6, being pulled from the blaze. They were the only sons of Marie Policard, 42, who was working at the time, and was devastated by her loss.

Blanc returned to the scene the next day and, with the permission of his superior officer, succeeded in raising funds for the boys' funeral and burial. But something was still missing: Policard's mother, Aurose Louis, grieved for her grandsons miles away in Haiti.

Again with his superior's okay, and helped by his girlfriend and community leaders, Blanc got inexpensive air tickets, boarded a flight to Port-au-Prince, and escorted the elderly woman to New York. "I didn't expect anything like this," she said later. "I really appreciate all that was done for me." And Marie Policard had the comfort of her mother in her hour of deepest need.

Let us love...in truth and action. (1 John 3:18)

May I be a comfort to those who grieve, Divine Consoler.

Bomb Technicians Make Easter Eggs

Every year for the past decade, visually impaired children have had the chance to hunt for Easter eggs, and they do it all on their own.

It began when David Hyche, a special agent with the Bureau of Alcohol, Tobacco and Firearms, discovered that his four-month-old daughter was blind. "With my daughter, one of her first phrases was, 'I do it myself,'" Hyche told *Fox News* at a 2015 egg hunt held in Birmingham, Alabama.

Hyche convinced the International Association of Bomb Technicians and Investigators to provide the funds to make beeping Easter eggs. And that was all it took for visually impaired kids to be able to engage in their own hunt.

Tamara Harrison of the Alabama Institute for the Deaf and Blind said, "We love to give the opportunity for our children with disabilities and their families to come out and have the same opportunity as everyone else."

For you shall go out in joy, and be led back in peace; the mountains and the hills before you shall burst into song, and all the trees of the field shall clap their hands. (Isaiah 55:12)

Lord, may the joy of children at play praise You always.

A Coach's Tips for Success

Legendary UCLA basketball coach John Wooden once offered these suggestions for achieving success in any endeavor.

- Fear no opponent.
- Remember, it's the perfection of the smallest detail that makes big things happen.
- Keep in mind that hustle makes up for many a mistake.
- Be more interested in character than reputation.
- Be quick, but don't hurry.
- Understand that the harder you work, the more luck you will have.
- Remember that there is no substitute for hard work and careful planning. Failing to prepare is preparing to fail.

Success means different things to different people. But we all have some particular desire, some goal we want to attain. Whether or not we are willing to work for it is up to us.

The Lord's...favor brings lasting success. (Sirach 11:17)

Give us success, Lord our God, and remind me to do my part in achieving it.

They Want to Live in Peace

"A Hindu, a Catholic, a Protestant, and a Jew all formed this committee [in Bahrain in the Middle East] and wanted me to come do a concert of peace," recalled singer-songwriter Michael W. Smith about a surprising invitation.

Bahrain is a predominantly Muslim country with many citizens of other faiths who want to build bridges of peace.

During an interview on *Christopher Closeup,* Smith said, "It was very, very shocking when I got the request that I'd been invited to Bahrain and been cleared by the king. It was one of the most memorable shows of my entire career. I met everybody on that committee and they genuinely, I think, really love each other, and they want to live in peace, and they don't want any blood shed on their streets, and they've learned how to live together. They can agree to disagree. We believe this, you believe that. They don't become radical about it to the point of taking somebody else's blood. Somehow they've figured out a way to live peacefully together."

May the rest of the world learn that lesson as well.

**Let each one go home in peace.
(2 Chronicles 18:16)**

Bless the efforts of all peacemakers, Creator.

The Real Patrick

The kidnapping of a teenage boy—the son of a deacon and grandson of a priest—1,600 years ago from what is now England, resulted in the Christianization of Ireland. That young man, Patricius, believed he was picked by God to return to the land of his enslavement.

Patricius became Patrick, and thanks to Thomas Cahill, author of *How the Irish Saved Civilization,* we know that Patrick is far more interesting than the legends about him. No, he didn't chase snakes out of Ireland.

What emerges from Patrick's own writing is humility and strength. "The Patrick who came back to Ireland with the gospel was tough...Only a very tough man could have hoped to survive those people," Cahill writes.

From St. Patrick we learn that saints are ordinary human beings with extraordinary toughness, vision and humility; that all life is worthy and precious; and that God has plans for us all.

My God, I seek You, my soul thirsts for You; my flesh faints for You. (Psalm 63:1)

Dear Lord, may my inner light and courage burn brightly.

Finding Security in Soybeans

It doesn't take much—sometimes just a simple soybean. That's what a farmer in Tanzania named Gertruda Domayo—who used to struggle to provide for her three grandchildren—found out. She joined a Catholic Relief Services project called Soya ni Pesa (which means "soybeans are money"), and her life changed. It turns out that soybeans really are money, and they paid her big benefits.

The Wooden Bell, CRS' magazine, reported not only that Domayo got lessons in crop spacing and fertilizer, which in turn doubled her harvests, but that membership in the farmers' group got her good prices at market. "And the soybeans themselves add nutrients to the soil," the story noted, "fueling future harvests."

By combining her crops with those of other farmers, Domayo now sells her soybeans in bulk. "Domayo's new way of selling," the magazine reported, "increased her income sixfold over the last year, when she sold her beans alone. Now she can afford to buy healthy food for her family."

She rises while it is still night and provides food for her household. (Proverbs 31:15)

Bless farmers with abundant crops, Creator.

The Other Papal City

A group of 12 seminarians from New York had the next best thing to a personal meeting with Pope Francis—a visit to Buenos Aires and an encounter with the city he knew so well, the people he served, and the priests with whom he worked.

For some, it was the experience of a lifetime. "I was so moved by all the people's stories about how the pope had in so many ways touched their lives," said seminarian Steven Gonzalez. "We could, in almost a tangible way, feel the pope's enormous impact and presence in a neighborhood."

While they were there, the seminarians helped to build a chapel on what had formerly been a garbage dump. They were impressed with the parish priests they met, following the example of the Jesuit priest who had once been their archbishop—before he was called to Rome.

"Working with the local people we were in some way able to meet the pope," seminarian Brian Muldoon recalled. "He walked the streets, knocked on doors. They knew him very personally."

Whoever walks with the wise becomes wise. (Proverbs 13:20)

May our actions bring us closer to Your divine love, Lord.

Finding Jesus in a POW Camp

Jacob DeShazer, a member of the U.S. Army Air Corps during World War II, was one of the Doolittle raiders who got captured by the Japanese after bombing their mainland.

DeShazer spent 40 months in a Japanese prisoner of war camp enduring horrific treatment, which included starvation, torture, lice, bedbugs, and rats. In addition, many of his fellow soldiers were executed or died from these deplorable conditions. The whole experience left DeShazer burning with hatred toward the Japanese, explained Daniel Fazzina in his book *Divine Intervention: 50 True Stories of God's Miracles Today.*

Somehow, a Bible made it into DeShazer's hands, so he read it constantly in his jail cell. Fazzina said, "He read that if you trust in the Lord, if you call upon the Lord, you shall be saved. He believed, and he gave his life to Jesus."

But could DeShazer take his conversion a step further and actually forgive the captors who were torturing him? We'll share the rest of the story tomorrow.

Your faith has saved you; go in peace. (Luke 7:50)

When suffering and loneliness are crushing my spirit, help me trust in You and renew my faith, Jesus.

Turning Hatred into Forgiveness

Jacob DeShazer may have given his life to God while in a Japanese POW camp during World War II, but could he go the extra mile and forgive his torturers? Daniel Fazzina, author of *Divine Intervention*, notes that DeShazer was especially struck by parts of the Bible where God calls us to love our enemies. His hatred for the Japanese eventually turned into forgiveness.

After the war ended and the prisoners were released, DeShazer returned home and promised God, "I'll go wherever You send me." He and his wife went back to Japan as missionaries, spending over 30 years there. His testimony was put on a tract in Japanese, and distributed throughout the country.

One of the people who read it was Captain Mitsuo Fuchida, who initiated the attack on Pearl Harbor. He bought a Bible out of curiosity, and eventually gave his life to Jesus. DeShazer and Fuchida actually became friends, ministering together in Japan, Hawaii, and elsewhere. Concludes Fazzina, "It's amazing how God can...bring two enemies together like that in the unity of the Holy Spirit."

Forgive the sin of Your people. (1 Kings 8:34)

Turn my resentments into forgiveness, Holy Spirit.

'We Need to Get Back Our Humanity'

In order to escape the brutality of ISIS terrorists, thousands of Iraqi men, women, and children fled their homes and headed to the northern Iraqi city of Erbil. Joining the refugees were the Dominican Sisters of St. Catherine of Siena, of which Sister Diana Momeka is a member.

The petite nun with a world-changing mission visited the New York office of the Catholic Near East Welfare Association (CNEWA) in 2015 to share her story. "People," she told Deacon Greg Kandra, "are living in slums. These people are human beings with great love, great faith. But when you lose your home, your heritage, your culture, you lose your dignity."

The Dominican Sisters are aiding the refugees by providing opportunities for medical care and education. Funds collected by CNEWA have helped tremendously. Sister Diana said, "This is how you care for the Body of Christ that has been hurting."

There is still much work to be done, however, in a situation that is far from safe. "We need to get back our humanity," said Sister Diana, "our human dignity."

I am persecuted without cause. (Psalm 119:86)

Protect the innocent victims of war from the evil that surrounds them, Father.

Taking the Long View

Oscar Romero, Archbishop of San Salvador, is hailed as a champion of the oppressed Salvadoran people. In fact, his opposition to injustice led to his assassination in 1980.

He understood the need—and the difficulty—of working for the future. But Archbishop Romero believed this: "It helps, now and then, to step back and take the long view...We accomplish in our lifetime only a tiny fraction of the magnificent enterprise that is the Lord's work.

"We plant the seeds that will one day grow, we water the seeds already planted knowing they hold future promise...We cannot do everything and there is a sense of liberation in realizing that. This enables us to do something, and to do it very, very well. It may be incomplete, but it is a beginning, a step along the way, an opportunity for the Lord's grace to enter and do the rest."

A generation goes, and a generation comes, but the earth remains forever. (Ecclesiastes 1:4)

Sometimes I need to be reminded that I may never see the end results of my efforts. Holy God, You are the Master Builder. I am Your worker, to labor as You ask.

From Anzio to Dodge City

In 1944, the U.S. Army 3rd Infantry Division stormed the beach in Anzio, Italy, and met fierce resistance from the German Army. Private James Aurness, a 20-year-old from Minneapolis, dodged oncoming bullets the best he could, but his six-foot-seven-inch frame made him an easy target. He suffered a serious wound in his knee and lower leg, earning a Bronze Star and Purple Heart for courage under fire.

Recovery and rehabilitation took 18 months, but Aurness would walk with a slight limp for the rest of his life. However, it didn't prevent him from changing his name to Arness, hitchhiking to Hollywood, and pursuing an acting career.

After landing roles in TV and film, he befriended actor John Wayne, who recommended him for the role of Marshall Matt Dillon in the TV series *Gunsmoke*. The show ran for 20 years, making Arness a star. But the humble actor never grew too big for his britches or forgot his past. Every year until his death in 2011, he and his wife Janet would visit California's Westwood military cemetery to pay their respects to the fallen.

Many are the afflictions of the righteous. (Psalm 34:19)

Guide the paths of all wounded warriors, Prince of Peace.

How Death Led to Faith

"If You save her life, I promise to dedicate my life to You."

At age 19, Nicole Lataif made that promise to God while riding the elevator at Boston Children's Hospital where her 12-year-old sister was a few hours away from succumbing to cancer.

Then, an instant later, Lataif changed her mind. Speaking out loud, she said, "Even if You don't save her life, I promise to dedicate my life to You." In a situation that might have driven some people away from believing in a loving God, Lataif's humility and faith grew stronger. They would grow even more when she and her parents sat with her sister on her deathbed, and her heartbroken mother said, "It's okay, go be with Jesus."

During a *Christopher Closeup* interview, Lataif recalled, "I felt like I was watching the Virgin Mary when she had to sacrifice her son in the same way...That defining moment was when I realized this life is not about me. It never was. And so, [my sister's] death led me to faith."

You are the one who lifts me up from the gates of death. (Psalm 9:13)

In times of suffering, Lord, protect my mind from despair and direct my soul toward Your healing comfort.

God Loves Us Back from the Edge

Kerry Weber received the call she had been dreading. Her sister's baby daughter had died only a few hours after being born due to developmental and health problems. Weber had prayed that the suffering of the baby and her sister could be transferred to herself, but she realized that's not how God works.

Writing in *America* magazine, Weber reflected, "We cannot always take away someone's suffering, but we can walk beside them, help them carry their burdens and in that way be able to walk farther together...Perhaps I can at least find a way to see the moments of joy in the pain, the grace and kindness of the doctors who treated my sister, the priest who slept in the hospital waiting room in order to baptize the baby at a moment's notice...

"During times of suffering, no matter how many times we are told that a resurrection is coming, it is tough to believe that we will emerge from the darkness...And so, instead of wondering why, we simply persevere, we try to find that joy, to let it transform us and to simply love our way through it all. Because even in our worst moments, this is what God does for us. God loves us back from the edge."

Your pain will turn into joy. (John 16:20)

Comfort those grieving the loss of a child, Father.

An Easter Testimony

It was Easter 2015 when singer-songwriter Brooke White decided to write about Jesus in a social media post. It wasn't something she had done much previously because she didn't want anyone to feel alienated if they believed differently than she does. Her faith, she hoped, would subtly shine through in her words. But because it was a special day, White decided, "Sometimes subtly isn't enough."

She went on to state, "I believe in Christ. For me, He's more than a regular guy, and the majority of who I am and the decisions I make are influenced by Him. His perfect understanding of the human condition helps me to overcome it.

"While my testimony has its fractures, it has survived natural disasters, attacks and the deepest of doubts. It amazes me how it still manages to function and thrive, because of the specific experiences where He's been there and made Himself known to me in indescribable and undeniable ways. For that, I'm massively grateful and loyal...Happy Easter!"

I am the resurrection and the life. Those who believe in Me, even though they die, will live. (John 11:25)

Give me the courage to share my faith in You, Jesus.

The Rock's Tender Side

Dwayne "The Rock" Johnson is known as a successful wrestler and actor with a "tough guy" image. But on Easter Sunday 2015, his tender side was on display after meeting a fan.

On his Facebook page, Johnson recalled leaving a workout session and driving away when he noticed several kids screaming and running after him. He stopped and got out of his truck to see what they wanted.

A young man named Nick Miller ran up to him, hugged him, and told him how much he'd inspired him to fight cancer. Miller revealed he had Hodgkin's lymphoma and was enduring chemotherapy along with stem cell transplant treatments.

Johnson wrote, "[Nick] was a little teary-eyed and said for months all he's wanted to do was find me and say this face-to-face. I told him what it meant to me to hear this story."

As Johnson drove away, he realized how appropriate this encounter was for Easter Sunday. It left him realizing how fragile life truly is and reminded him to count his blessings.

Health and fitness are better than any gold. (Sirach 30:15)

Bring hope and healing to cancer victims, Divine Healer.

My Uncle's a Saint...Really

Everyone has a "sainted" aunt or uncle; an unusually good person, perhaps, who always managed to do the right thing. "Aunt Edna was a saint," someone will declare, and heads will nod in agreement as a pious relative is recalled. And that's that.

Father Luigi Esposito, on the other hand, is something else. When he refers to "my uncle, the saint," he's not kidding. His great-great uncle, St. Ludovico of Casoria (1814-1885), was canonized in 2014 and was known for his dedication to the poor, to orphans and the elderly.

Father Esposito, pastor of Our Lady of Pompei in Highlandtown, Maryland, recalls attending the 1993 beatification with a relative. "When they uncovered the picture of St. Ludovico," he said, "both my cousin and myself started crying, because we recognized the family features." The saint and his own uncle, Father Esposito recalled, "could have been twins."

And there was something else. "He was a handsome man, apparently," he joked to Erik Zygmont of the *Catholic Review*. "He would have to be, being part of the family."

**You are a people holy to the Lord.
(Deuteronomy 7:6)**

You call all people to sainthood, Lord. Show us the way.

Taking the High Road

Remember Mo'ne Davis? She's the young lady from Philadelphia who stole America's heart by hurling a no-hitter in the 2014 Little League World Series. She was in the news again last year when a collegian from Pennsylvania wrote some very unladylike things about her on his Twitter post, and was bounced from the Bloomsburg University baseball team as a result.

At first, Mo'ne tried to laugh off the comments in the student's tweet, but when she saw the attention it was getting, "it kind of hurt." So what did she do? She wrote to Bloomsburg and asked that he be reinstated—"because he shouldn't have his life ruined because of one lapse in judgment."

As Mo'ne told Wayne Coffey of New York's *Daily News*, "Even though what he did was really hurtful, I thought about how hard he probably worked to get to be a college player. It was a really big mistake, but we all make mistakes."

The head of Mo'ne's school saw it coming. "It doesn't surprise me that Mo'ne would take the high road," said Priscilla Sands. "It's who she is."

You have dealt with us according to your great mercy. (Tobit 8:16)

Free our hearts from bitterness, Prince of Peace.

Mini's Mission

Virginia native Timmy Tyrell turns 10 this year. But the highlight of his birthday isn't the number of presents he receives. Rather, he's more interested in the number of donations made to his charity, Mini's Mission.

Timmy's nonprofit, which to date has raised a quarter of a million dollars, was founded three years ago, when the six-year-old discovered his friend Ella was diagnosed with cancer. Any funds from Mini's Mission helped Ella's family pay for her exorbitant medical bills.

Timmy's fledgling charity has since grown to include the financial aid of professional NASCAR driver Jeff Gordon, who heads his own foundation for children with cancer. Both Timmy and his father, also named Timmy, hold racing records as well. In fact, at the ripe age of eight, Timmy, nicknamed Mini, became the youngest winner in Arena Car Race history.

"Never in our wildest imagination, could we have predicted what Mini would accomplish in just three years," Timmy's mother, Tina, told *NBC Nightly News*. "He's not only inspiring adults. He's also inspiring young kids."

Train children in the right way. (Proverbs 22:6)

God, protect and guide all children, life's greatest legacy.

Christmas in April

For some people, Santa Claus arrives in early Spring. He exchanges his red suit and sleigh for a hammer and nails—and rather than sliding down the chimney, he's busy fixing it.

These industrious Santas are members of Christmas in April, a national volunteer organization that helps low-income homeowners fix their houses. If the owners meet federal poverty guidelines and organizational criteria, 20 to 25 volunteers launch a one-day mission of repair.

The program is a joint effort of private citizens and corporate sponsors. While volunteers perform all the actual repairs, local building-supply companies provide the materials and nearby restaurants provide workers with food. Houses that were unsafe and in disrepair are transformed into welcoming homes, but the real achievements are the bonds that form when neighbors work together for a common cause.

Money is not always the answer. We can give of our hearts, heads and hands too.

Every house is built by someone, but the builder of all things is God. (Hebrews 3:4)

Carpenter of Nazareth, teach me to build with the gifts You have given me.

Joy in the Rain

The downpour began just as Sirius-XM radio host Leah Darrow and her children got home from their walk, so they rushed for cover in the garage. After taking her daughter Agnes out of her stroller, the little girl walked into the rain and started smiling and dancing around.

Darrow's initial inclination was to bring Agnes back into the garage, but as she wrote on the social media website Instagram, she found the girl's smile "mesmerizing" and didn't want to end her moment of happiness.

Darrow continued, "This made me think of our relationship with God. Sometimes His immense and infinite love and mercy is alarming. Can He really love me that much? Will He forgive me? Yet at times, it seems when we need His mercy the most, fear takes over and we run for cover—away from Him.

"But Agnes made me think that maybe we should run *to* God's love and mercy like she runs into the rain. To let ourselves be free in Him and allow His love and mercy to shower us—to replenish and renew our souls."

He will renew you in His love. (Zephaniah 3:17)

Father, open my heart to life's simple joys.

The Quality of Mercy

The works of William Shakespeare are quoted on an amazing variety of subjects because of their wisdom and beauty.

These are his most famous words on mercy:

"The quality of mercy is not strained. It droppeth as the gentle rain from heaven upon the place beneath.

"It is twice blest: It blesseth him that gives and him that takes. 'Tis mightiest in the mightiest. Mercy is an attribute of God Himself...Earthly power does show like God's when mercy seasons justice."

This is one excerpt from Portia's speech in *The Merchant of Venice*. You may benefit from contemplating those words. You know Jesus said, "Blessed are the merciful for they shall receive mercy." Is there anyone who needs your mercy today?

The Lord is merciful...abounding in steadfast love. (Psalm 103:8)

May I be as merciful as You are, Lover of Souls.

Beauty Appreciated and Ignored

One April morning, New Yorkers passing a small park were stopped by its beauty. Two cherry trees were in full bloom. The wind was sending their pink petals swirling through the air like pink snow, covering the sidewalks. In the background, a waterfall sparkled in the sun.

Many workers on their way to offices paused to enjoy the sight. But not the park attendant. Armed with a broom and dustpan, he frantically tried to sweep up petals as they floated down.

The expression on his face made it clear that he saw the delicate beauty only as litter that would have to be tossed out with the trash. He completely missed the fleeting, fragile moment of beauty the petals provided.

Undue concern about finishing our "to do" lists can often blind us to the beauty in front of us right now. Yes, we all have obligations. But we also have moments to appreciate. They are just as real and just as important.

Today's trouble is enough for today.
(Matthew 6:34)

Help me enjoy the present rather than worry about the next hour, day, week, month or year, Lord, to whom belongs all time and all the seasons.

Be a Better Listener

Being a good listener can benefit your home life, your career, and your relationships, so professional counselor Julia Hogan offered some tips in *Verily* magazine:

- **Limit your distractions.** Silence or put away your cell phone for the duration of your conversation or meeting.

- **Adjust your body language.** "Face the person speaking while leaning slightly forward. Make frequent eye contact. Nod your head to signal understanding, and maintain an open posture (that means no crossed arms!)."

- **Do a double-check.** "Ask clarifying questions and paraphrase what the speaker just communicated to you. [And] be sure to ask open-ended questions...These types of questions help deepen conversation and elicit key details."

- **Avoid being solution-focused.** "Sometimes, people just want a chance to talk through an issue instead of identifying a solution right away. It's important to validate your friend's feelings. Try, 'That must have been so frustrating!' Then you'll have a better idea of what solutions you can offer if necessary."

Speak, Lord...Your servant is listening. (1 Samuel 3:9)

Holy Spirit, teach me to be a better listener.

Prayer and Cattle

At the foot of the Colorado Rockies rests the Abbey of St. Walburga, which houses a cloistered group of Benedictine nuns. In addition to a life of prayer, they also run a self-sustaining farm on their 250 acres of land. That farm has grown to include an increasingly-thriving natural beef business.

NBC News's Erica Hill reported that the nuns hadn't planned on selling beef, but people kept asking about it because their cattle were raised in a healthy way. Hill said, "Last year, St. Walburga produced 13,000 pounds of naturally-raised beef for 80 local families—and that still doesn't meet the demand."

Sister Maria-Walburga Schortemeyer says the farm work complements their spirituality: "Having an agrarian part of our life keeps us rooted to the earth...We try hard to run it in a reverent way. The animals are treated with care."

However, she never loses sight of their real goal: "We're not blind, even in our enclosure, to the great sorrows that many people experience. I believe...that through prayer we can have an impact."

You cause the grass to grow for the cattle. (Psalm 104:14)

Bless farmers and all efforts to feed the hungry, Lord.

Joy is a Rebellion Against the World

There aren't a lot of rock albums out there that were partially inspired by theologian G.K. Chesterton, so Jonathan Jackson and his band Enation have created something unique.

Jackson is an actor known for his work on *General Hospital* and *Nashville,* but he is also a longtime musician who created the band Enation with his brother Richard Lee and their friend Daniel Sweatt. One of the common threads in their songwriting is spiritual depth, and that's especially true of their latest album *Radio Cinematic.*

During a *Christopher Closeup* interview, Jonathan said the new record was inspired by Chesterton's idea that God invites us to enter a second childhood as we get older and claim a new sense of joy in life: "Growing up, the world has its way of beating you down. So in the band, we've always seen joy and hope as a kind of rebellion. It's not this passive, soft thing that people oftentimes think. It actually comes from having to fight."

God wants you to be joyful. Claim that special gift.

A cheerful heart is a good medicine, but a downcast spirit dries up the bones. (Proverbs 17:22)

Preserve me from giving in to cynicism, Lord. Help me fight to reclaim Your joy.

Escaping a War Zone

"How long shall it be till the end of these troubles?" That's a quote from the Book of Daniel that's spoken by a refugee from the Sudanese Civil War in the movie *The Good Lie*—and it accurately reflects the violence and hardship endured by boys and girls there throughout those horrific times.

During the mid-1980s, more than 100,000 children in Sudan were displaced or orphaned because of the civil war that raged for political and religious reasons. Many of them found their way to refugee camps and, eventually, the United States.

Screenwriter Margaret Nagle not only talked with refugees, but also interviewed volunteers, pastors, and church leaders who helped these young people. And producer Brian Grazer said, "Around the time we were making the movie, I brought my kids to an orphanage in Kenya because I wanted them to understand and appreciate the freedoms and privileges they have in their lives. I think that's one of the things our film speaks to: being grateful and thanking God for what we have. And perhaps to ignite something in us to help where we can, however we can."

He fled away and escaped. (1 Samuel 19:12)

Guide those fleeing violence to safety, Divine Wisdom.

Zach's Shack

When Zach Francom was eight years old, he opened up his own lemonade and cookie stand, called Zach's Shack. While he isn't the first boy to have a lemonade stand, he does stand out because he gives his proceeds to those who cannot afford to buy a wheelchair. The child got the idea when his class raised $86 to donate to LDS Philanthropies, a charity that provides wheelchairs for people in developing countries who need them.

What started out as a simple gesture of altruism on Zach's part has evolved into an annual philanthropic event for the past four years. Every April, hundreds of people line up in front of Zach's Shack in Provo, Utah, to donate to his cause. He only charges 50 cents for a glass of lemonade, and a dollar per cookie, but it all adds up. In April 2015, Zach raised $5,300, enough to purchase 37 wheelchairs. The youngster hopes his organization will keep growing.

"Imagine if there were hundreds of Zach's Shacks," Zach told *People* magazine. "Nobody who needs a wheelchair should have to go without one just because they can't afford it."

**Whoever gives...will lack nothing.
(Proverbs 28:27)**

Lord, may we learn from the selfless giving of our children.

Keys to Longevity?

Many people are living to age 100 and beyond—hopefully with health, happiness and a positive outlook. Dora Gianniello is one such senior, who was thrilled to reach her 100th birthday on Tax Day, April 15th. According to the *Staten Island Advance*, "she hails from a fun-loving family, who always loved bringing smiles to others."

On the West coast, the local newspaper in Victoria, California, featured Ovie Corrington in a story titled "Centenarian Shares Her Recipe for Longevity." She is known for her strong heart, deep faith and contagious joy.

Naturally, she has endured struggles, but "Corrington said she attributes her ability to continue on and reach 100 years to three basic ingredients: her love for Jesus, laughter, and 'simply enjoying what you had to do for your family and for others.'"

Not everyone is blessed with a caring family, strong psychological constitution or good genes. So let's pitch in and offer support when we notice unmet needs.

By Me your days will be multiplied, and years will be added to your life. (Proverbs 9:11)

May I choose the right ingredients for a happy life, Lord.

Everyone's Contributions Are Needed

"Human suffering and despair are present in all corners of the globe," notes Rev. Dr. Lisa W. Davison on the *Sojourners* magazine blog. So how do we deal with all of this pain? The story of Jean Vanier provides an answer.

Vanier started a movement called L'Arche "by simply inviting mentally disabled friends to share his home," writes Rev. Davison. "Vanier was recently awarded the 2015 Templeton Prize...given to a living individual who has made an important contribution toward the spiritual dimension of life."

She continued, "As the founder of L'Arche, a network of 147 communities around the world in which persons of differing intellectual abilities live and work together, Vanier has made his life work about creating inclusive communities that honor the divine in each person."

Imagine if we all took a little initiative to honor the divine in each person. On second thought, don't just imagine it. Do it.

I will...gather the outcast. (Zephaniah 3:19)

Help us, Lord, to appreciate and value how our contributions can make the world a better place.

The Wife Who Wouldn't Give Up

Matt Davis of Savannah, Georgia, was in a motorcycle accident in July 2011 that left him with such severe brain damage that doctors advised his wife, Danielle, to take him off life support. They had been married for only seven months.

Danielle said of her 22-year-old husband, "I wanted to give him more time to see if he improved. We didn't really have a chance to start our life together. I wasn't going to give up."

Danielle brought Matt home, where she and her mother cared for him. They noticed he was trying to talk, and one day Danielle held his hat out and told him to grab it. After multiple tries, he finally gasped, "I'm trying!" Recalling that moment, she exclaimed, "It was the greatest thing I've ever heard!"

In 2015, *ABC News* reported on Matt's progress. He is working on walking, can drive a stick shift, crack jokes and play Scrabble. One of the lasting effects of his brain injury is memory loss, so he doesn't remember Danielle from before the accident. But, he says, "I'm sure glad I married her."

Love...endures all things. (1 Corinthians 13:7)

Lord, may married couples be true to each other in sickness and health.

Remembering the Doolittle Raid

Americans old enough to remember the Doolittle Raid in April of 1942 recall the incredible lift it gave to the nation's morale. Until then the U.S. had been suffering through the early and dark days of World War II, when the news was universally bad and the Japanese foe seemed to be winning every battle.

Suddenly the war was brought directly to the Japanese homeland, to Tokyo and other major cities, by the heroism of a handful of men. American spirits soared as 16 B-25s took off from the USS Hornet, dropped their bombs on Japan, and proceeded toward uncertain fates in China.

Last year, only three men were left of the 90 who had taken part in the original mission, which was under the command of Lt. Col. James "Jimmy" Doolittle, later a brigadier general. And they were still being honored: the group received the Congressional Gold Medal in Washington. At age 99, Lt. Col. Richard Cole said from his Texas home that he planned to attend, on behalf of all his fellow veterans. Those who recall the event might be dwindling—but a nation has never forgotten.

Be strong and courageous...the Lord your God is with you wherever you go. (Joshua 1:9)

Bring veterans the peace they deserve, Lord.

Resuscitating a Life

Talk about being in the right place at the right time! That's the story of Fernando Frias, 32, a rookie member of the New York Fire Department's emergency medical technician team. He was about to wind up one of his first shifts when a man flagged down his ambulance. Frias said, "He's telling me to come to this restaurant; there's a man there who needs help."

The man sure did. He was Gabriel Hernandez, 54, a radio host in the Dominican Republic. One minute he was chatting with friends, and the next he was collapsed on the floor. "I'm thinking, I'm brand new; I don't know what's going on," Frias said. "I've got to stay calm. I had to go back to my training."

It took a half-hour of resuscitation, the *Daily News* reported, but then Hernandez revived—and now he's fine. He thanked Frias in person at a ceremony that reunited EMT workers with the people they saved—and the New Yorker was sure that he never had a warmer word of thanks.

God is our refuge and strength, a very present help in trouble. (Psalm 46:1)

May my presence be a saving grace for someone in trouble, Divine Healer.

Retiring...Sort Of

Life may not begin at 90 for Sister Ann Michele Jadlowski, but it's sure time to keep going. She's still taking care of people in St. Paul, Minnesota, at St. Joseph Hospital, founded by her order, the Sisters of St. Joseph of Carondelet. "Our mission here," she explained, "is to continue the mission of our sisters, which was compassion to anyone who comes to our doors."

Sister Ann Michele "sort of" retired from the spirituality department at the hospital when she turned 85, but as she told Jessica Trygstad of *The Catholic Spirit*, she felt good enough to keep at it. She is the only sister left at the hospital, now part of the HealthEast Care System.

"I think about the people I've met and the people I know, and it's very enriching," Sister Ann Michele said. "I know I have been given the gift of being able to listen and being compassionate. So, what keeps me here is knowing where I came from, knowing the experience I've had, and knowing about what I need to try to help to keep that going."

Many years teach wisdom. (Job 32:7)

Christ, guide our society toward valuing the gift of seniors still willing and able to share their gifts with the world.

Nobody's Perfect

Rabbi Harold Kushner visited a dying man and asked if he was angry at God for what was happening to him. "No," the man replied, "There have been many times when I felt God had given up on me. But lying here in the hospital, I've felt God's presence."

"When I was young," the man continued, "I thought I had to be perfect for people to love me. So every time I did something wrong, I would make excuses. I would try to find someone else to blame. I didn't realize what an unpleasant person I became when I acted that way.

"I thought it was my imperfection, not my defensiveness, that turned people off. But I've finally learned that you don't have to be perfect to be worth loving. I only wish I had learned that sooner."

The words of a man at the end of his life give each of us a lesson for every day of life.

I have loved you with an everlasting love; therefore I have continued my faithfulness to you. (Jeremiah 31:3)

You alone, Lord, are perfect. Stay by my side as I travel life's rough road.

Good Mental Health in a Stressful World

In today's increasingly stressful world, it's important to maintain a peaceful body and spirit. In a recent issue of *The Beacon*, former Christophers' Director Father John Catoir offered some useful mental health tips:

- **You are not your thoughts.** Don't let dark thoughts define you. Remember, God is stronger than any evil, real or imagined.

- **Work to control your temper.** Anger is like a poisonous acid, doing far more damage to its container than on what it is poured.

- **Be grateful for every blessing, however small**.

- **Work is good for the body.** Whether it's at school or work, always put your best foot forward.

- **Choose joy over sorrow.** Happiness is a conscious decision we need to make every day, for the good of ourselves and others.

- **Cheerfulness is a key ingredient of good health.** You'd be surprised at how helping others can lift your own spirits.

- **Stop and think.** We cannot control the circumstances in our lives, only our reactions to those circumstances.

Peace I leave with you, My peace I give...you. (John 14:27)

Divine Savior, heal us of our infirmities.

Father Damien's Way

One of the country's easternmost dioceses got together with one from the far, far west last year to honor a famed missionary saint.

Patrick Downes of the *Hawaii Catholic Herald* reported that New York has renamed a section of East 33rd Street in Manhattan for Saint Damien, the Belgian-born priest who ministered to patients with Hansen's disease (also known as leprosy) on the island of Molokai in Hawaii.

"Father Damien Way" occupies the section of 33rd Street between First and Second avenues, home of the Sacred Hearts of Jesus and Mary parish. Saint Damien, a 19th-century missionary who was canonized in 2009, was a member of the congregation of the Sacred Hearts.

Two residents of Kalaupapa, site of the original hospital established by Saint Damien for treatment of those with Hansen's disease, led the delegation from Hawaii who attended the ceremony. Saint Damien, who eventually contracted the disease, died as a result of its complications on April 15, 1889.

**Cure the sick...cleanse the lepers.
(Matthew 10:8)**

Divine Healer, open our hearts to caring for society's outcasts with Christ-like compassion.

RE:PODS

Six years ago, Carey Warren and Brian Barger set out to "create clean, renewable energy from organic waste." Their time-consuming efforts led them through experiences with "crazy inventors, fraudulent technology, bad partners," and more.

In 2015, their work finally paid off when they closed a deal "on the exclusive licensing of gasification technology from Oklahoma State University."

On his Facebook page, Warren explained, "This machine—and our company—is named RE:PODS: Renewable Energy Power On Demand Systems. Our first unit will be finished by the end of the summer. Our market consists of any place on the planet with too much trash and not enough power: disaster areas, refugee camps, hospitals...Once we're funded, we will only manufacture in the United States, and we will specifically look to hire U.S. veterans and skilled American workers."

Ingenuity and determination can lead not only to strong businesses, but to the creation of a better world.

We will reap at harvest time, if we do not give up. (Galatians 6:9)

May I be persistent in my efforts to do good, Lord.

Why I'm Thankful

The inspirational newsletter *Apple Seeds* shared a prayer about gratitude that stemmed from Catholic Relief Services. Here is an excerpt: "Lord of Life, They ask me why I stop to pray and begin my prayers with thanks in a world fraught with pain and loss, with cruelty and injustice. Sometimes I ask myself this too. And then I look again and gratitude fills my heart anew.

"Because when somebody is hungry, another is dividing their portion. When somebody is thirsty, another is digging a well...Because when disaster strikes and people flee, somebody else—against all sense—is running toward the danger...to reach out Your saving hand to an absolute stranger. And when somebody dies, somebody else stops to pray, and then makes a home for the orphan.

"It's as confounding as it is beautiful. In this darkened world, where the face of God is veiled in the midst of calamities, when all instinct speaks of self-preservation, somebody still cares for the other and miracles of compassion abound. This is why I'm thankful. Amen."

Give thanks in all circumstances.
(1 Thessalonians 5:18)

Strengthen my sense of gratitude, Prince of Peace.

The Kindness of Fellow Flyers

Credit frequent flyer Jim O'Connell of Ridgewood, New Jersey, with a sensitivity that should endear him to countless friends of The Christophers. In a regular weekly feature in *The New York Times*, travelers such as O'Connell are asked, among other things, to name their favorite airports and why they like them. To things like frequent flights or ease of maneuverability, O'Connell added a surprising reason for appreciating just about any airport he's come across: the kindness of fellow flyers.

"One of the most gracious, kind acts I saw," he wrote, "was a woman who actually gave up her seat on a sold-out flight after hearing a man pleading with the gate attendant. He needed to get home because of a family emergency." O'Connell also told of a "kindly, older man" who came to the aid of another passenger: an overwhelmed father, without his wife, with three crying children in tow. The man helped settle the children down by offering a few kind words.

"It was a great moment," O'Connell concludes, "and proves that not everyone is miserable when flying. Some people still remember that kindness goes a long way."

You showed kindness to Your people. (Wisdom 16:2)

Lord, may I always remember to practice kindness.

Flowers Outside the Box

Although Jim McCann's initial career direction was uncertain, he encountered people who planted seeds in his mind which ultimately blossomed into a very successful career.

McCann hadn't been a serious student until he met an inspirational teacher at CUNY/John Jay College of Criminal Justice, who encouraged him to think "outside the box."

"I met this teacher named Blanche Cook who stormed into our class with knee-high boots and a lot of in-your-face attitude and made you rethink the way you thought about the world," he told Denis Hamill of New York's *Daily News.*

At the same time that he was a student, McCann met a florist who wanted to sell his shop. After a trial period, McCann decided to buy the business and an under-utilized 800 number. He transformed it into 1-800-Flowers. Now company CEO, McCann invited Cook to be his guest at John Jay College's 50th anniversary dinner because of the difference she made in his life.

All of us can plant seeds today to bear fruit in the future.

I will instruct you and teach you the way you should go. (Psalm 32:8)

Bless our teachers, Abba, and all who inspire us to make a difference.

The Matheny Manifesto

As the father of five children who were active in sports, St. Louis Cardinals' manager Mike Matheny had seen his share of out-of-control parents at his kids' games. After being asked to coach his young son's baseball team, he wrote a letter to parents spelling out his expectations. It soon became known as The Matheny Manifesto. Here are a few points:

- "I believe that the biggest role of the parent [at games] is to be a silent source of encouragement... It's hard not to coach from the stands and yell things, but trust me: Coaching and yelling works against their development and enjoyment."

- "A large part of how your child improves is your responsibility... You can help out tremendously [at home] by playing catch, throwing batting practice, hitting ground balls."

- "The boys will be required to show up ready to play every time they come to the field. Shirts tucked in, hats on straight, and pants not drooping down to their knees. There is not an excuse for lack of hustle on a baseball field...Players that do not hustle and run out balls will not play."

**Athletes exercise self-control in all things.
(1 Corinthians 9:25)**

Lord, help us to instill our youth with a sense of diligence and responsibility.

Forever and Ever, Amen

Christina Capecchi, whose syndicated column graces the pages of many Catholic newspapers, tells the story of Joseph and Helen Auer of Cincinnati, married for an incredible 73 years. When Helen died in the fall of 2014, Joe kissed her and whispered, "Mama, call me home." She answered his request almost at once. Joe passed away 28 hours later, at the age of 100.

Capecchi said their Catholic faith undergirded their union. "It was like oatmeal," she wrote, "giving them sustenance. It was like a full daily planner, lending them purpose. It was like stardust, offering them hope."

Joe missed the birth of his second child while fighting in World War II, but there were more kids to come—10 in all. The Auers endured hardships—"a night job, farm chores, miscarriages, Catholic-school tuition"—by attending Mass, going to confession weekly and praying a nightly rosary.

One daughter said, "They always put God first," and a grandson—one of 16 grandchildren—recalls the mandates with which he grew up: "work hard, finish your meal, say please, go to church." As legacies go, they don't come much better.

Love never ends. (1 Corinthians 13:8)

Give married couples the grace to thrive, Father.

The Wright Response to a City's Loss

David Wright comes through again for the New York Mets! The slugging third baseman, son of a Virginia police officer, took the lead in arranging a special day for the families of two slain New York policemen last year.

Patrolmen Rafael Ramos and Wenjian Liu were killed as they sat in their squad car in December of 2014. The *Daily News* established a fund which raised $700,000, and the presentation of that check was part of the ceremonies as the Mets hosted some 20 of the policemen's family and friends. But the emphasis was on the day itself, a day the families enjoyed. That was particularly true for Justin and Jaden Ramos, sons of one of the police officers—and dedicated Mets fans.

"This has been an awesome experience," said Justin, a sophomore at Bowdoin College in Maine. Wright was lavish in his praise, too. "For me it was more important just to express my condolences," he said. "To let them know that their father was a hero, and they have an open invitation to come down here whenever they'd like to."

Cast your burden on the Lord, and He will sustain you. (Psalm 55:22)

Bring healing to the families of fallen police officers, Jesus.

Clearing Clutter

If you've been putting off clearing out the clutter in your home, here are some ideas from a time management expert.

Get some big cardboard boxes and label them:

- **Trash:** for those things of no use to you or anybody else.
- **Charity:** for items useful to others.
- **Posterity:** for sentimental items.
- **Transition:** for things that need to be sorted through carefully.

Then go to work, one room at a time, or even one drawer at a time. Approaching any goal just one step at a time rather than worrying about doing everything completely and perfectly is a sound idea.

Add persistence to a well-thought-out plan and you may accomplish more than you thought possible.

**Better is a little with the fear of the Lord than great treasure and trouble with it.
(Proverbs 15:16)**

Jesus, enable me to simplify my life, not just my home, so that reverence for You may be my chief priority.

Lonely Seeker of Comfort

A woman from Halifax, Nova Scotia, described her experience when she went to a local church for the first time. A widow, she had moved to a smaller house in a new town where she found herself overwhelmed by loneliness.

She hadn't been to church since she was a little girl, but hoped she might find solace. There wasn't a crowd at the service and everyone seemed to know and talk to everyone else.

Because the newcomer didn't know the liturgy, she kept glancing at others to see if she was standing or kneeling at the right times. At the end, she walked slowly back down the aisle, hoping someone would say hello. They didn't. Even "the Vicar was shaking hands with people...but somehow I seemed to get missed."

Don't let someone "get missed." Reach out. It can be as simple as a smile and a word of welcome. We need one another.

What does the Lord require of you but to do justice, and to love kindness. (Micah 6:8)

You've never ignored me, Lord. May I never ignore anyone.

Wired for Kindness

A recent series of studies from the University of British Columbia suggests "we come into this world wired to prefer kindness," reports Daniel Goleman in the *Washington Post*.

The studies involve showing infants and toddlers a puppet show that includes a kind character and a mean one. Between 80 to 100 percent of the children express a liking for the kind one.

Though "research shows that as they enter school around age five or so, children shift away from their innate altruism toward selfishness," that inclination can be neutralized by re-enforcing the benefits of kindness. That supports the opinion of the Dalai Lama, who Goleman interviewed for his book *A Force for Good*. "Compassion, he says—and science agrees—is innate, and can be strengthened like a muscle."

Since we are all made in the image and likeness of God, we all inherently share in a measure of God's love and kindness. By building up those natural qualities in ourselves, we can grow to be even more like Him.

Be perfect, therefore, as your heavenly Father is perfect. (Matthew 5:48)

Guide me toward choosing kindness every day, Father.

Breaking Bad vs. Choosing Good

Best-selling novelist and Catholic convert Dean Koontz tends to write about people who choose evil after bad things have happened in their past. At the same time, some people deal with adversity and emerge more compassionate. Why does he think some people break bad, while others get better?

During a *Christopher Closeup* interview, Koontz said, "I think that it comes back to believing in something bigger than us. If you find that very difficult, then you fall into nihilism. You think it doesn't matter what you do because the world is just a chaotic place and nothing has any meaning. But if you're aware that things do have meaning, the evidence is everywhere.

"I don't think you have to be religious in the sense of a churchgoer and be a member of a particular creed. You can look around the world without having been raised that way and with your eyes wide open and you will see almost daily so many strangenesses and mysteries...That's something that's been with me since I was a kid: this sense of wonder about the world—and it only grows richer for me the older I get."

The heavens are telling the glory of God. (Psalm 19:1)

Open my eyes, mind and heart to Your wonders, Creator.

Forgiving the Unforgivable

One of the biggest recent decisions in Lisa Hendey's life was traveling to Rwanda with Catholic Relief Services on a journalism fellowship. It was the 20th anniversary of the Rwandan genocide in which close to one million people were murdered, often in "neighbor-on-neighbor" violence.

During a *Christopher Closeup* interview, Hendey recalled, "We were meeting with genocide perpetrators and survivors and reconciliation groups to look at how they've moved forward as a society and found forgiveness. When I would listen to them discuss the ability to strive for forgiveness, it made me realize how many things I carry around in my own heart that separate me from union with God.

"I'm sometimes carrying these burdens of terrible grudges against people who don't even know that I'm angry with them! And when I refuse to give forgiveness, it doesn't hurt the other person, it hurts me and my relationship with God. [Also], if these people in Rwanda can forgive the unforgivable, how amazing is it that there's a God who forgives me of all the things that I do."

Forgive the iniquity of this people according to the greatness of Your steadfast love. (Numbers 14:19)

Open my heart to forgiveness, Father.

Are You a Lovin' Spoonful?

Kayleen J. Reusser wrote a letter to *The Christian Reader* about an experience with her daughter, Lindsay.

The seven-year-old was helping her mom set the table. "I'm glad I'm not a fork," she announced.

"What's wrong with forks?" asked her mom.

"Forks like to stab things, trying to get everything for themselves. It's like they say, 'Gimme, gimme' all the time."

Her mom asked her if she preferred knives. "Too bossy," said Lindsay. "Knives always want to change things to fit themselves."

She picked up a spoon. "But spoons are like your friends," she said. "They don't try to change anything. They just seem to say, 'Here, let me help you.'"

Reflecting on her daughter's introspection, Reusser writes, "God wants us to be like that, serving others with a kind spirit."

Those who are kind reward themselves, but the cruel do themselves harm. (Proverbs 11:17)

Kind Jesus, remind us that kindness always counts.

Finding Guidance in the Ceramics Shop

John Schlimm spent his 20s working in public relations for the White House, and then, for country music stars in Nashville. From a worldly perspective, he had it made. Yet, at age 31, he felt restless and empty. His quest for meaning led him to leave his job and return to his hometown of St. Marys, Pennsylvania.

One day, Schlimm visited a small ceramics shop on the grounds of St. Joseph Monastery, which was home to the Benedictine Sisters of Elk County. That's where he met 87-year-old Sister Augustine, who single-handedly ran the ceramics shop and created all its pieces of art.

Schlimm noticed a palpable joy in her personality, which was ironic since he used to work with people who had the world at their fingertips yet struggled to find happiness. In contrast, here was a cloistered nun in an out-of-the-way ceramics shop who was totally happy and content. Schlimm sensed that she might be able to guide him toward that deeper fulfillment for which he was looking. And that's exactly what she did.

More of the story tomorrow.

**Strive first for the kingdom of God.
(Matthew 6:33)**

Guide my restless heart to better knowing You, Jesus.

Five Years in Heaven

During one of John Schlimm's visits with Sister Augustine, she talked about the joys and sorrows that are involved in making ceramics. As Schlimm recalled during a *Christopher Closeup* interview about his memoir *Five Years in Heaven: The Unlikely Friendship That Answered Life's Greatest Questions,* he said, "I once asked her what it was like to open the kiln and see all of these incredible pieces that she had created. She smiled and said, 'Every time I open the kiln, there's joys and sorrows'—meaning that some of the pieces [will] be shattered.

"The point she made was that even those sorrows are moments for us to pause and be grateful. With every shard of broken ceramic, she picks it up and says, 'Thank you, God.' [I thought], 'That's not something I really want to be given as a gift: a sorrow.' But she changed my mind on that and showed how those sorrows and challenges in life, we can either see them as a roadblock or as an amazing gift to go in a new direction."

More of the story tomorrow.

All things work together for good. (Romans 8:28)

Lord, when sorrows threaten my spirit, give me the strength to believe in Your positive plan for me.

Learning From Your Elders

John Schlimm's friendship with Sister Augustine taught him about the way our youth-oriented society treats the elderly.

He said, "I was fortunate to grow up around my elderly grandparents—and my parents taught me a respect for older people, so I was comfortable with them. Unfortunately today, kids aren't really around people who are in their 70s, 80s and 90s, so they don't know how to connect with them. We need to become more comfortable reaching out to them, because in so many cases, our elderly fall by the wayside. We have so much to learn from them, and we're starting to lose that!"

Readers of Schlimm's book *Five Years in Heaven* now approach him all the time saying, "I wish I had a Sister Augustine in my life." His response to them?

"You probably do. If you look around, it might be the old guy down the street who waves at you every time you pass his house or the grandmother you don't get to visit enough. Connect with these people and ask them lots of questions."

Rich experience is the crown of the aged. (Sirach 25:6)

Creator, lead me toward senior citizens willing to share their rich life experiences with me.

Listening Heart-to-Heart

This story was told more than seven centuries ago by the Persian poet Attar: A sick man was weeping bitterly. Someone asked him, "Why are you crying?" The sick man answered, "I am crying to attract the pity of God's heart."

The other said, "You are talking nonsense, for God doesn't have a physical heart." The sick man replied, "It's you who are wrong. He is the owner of all the hearts that exist. It's through the heart that you can make your connection with God."

This story's message still speaks to people of all faiths. When our hearts are open to the needs of others, we can become the instrument of God's help to them. We often have to listen for the feeling behind a person's words or behavior. A friend or family member who lashes out with angry words for no apparent reason may be saying, "Things are rough for me right now, and the pain is more than I can cope with." A child who misbehaves may be trying to get attention because he or she feels neglected.

Become a channel of God's love.

O Lord my God, I cried to You for help, and You have healed me. (Psalm 30:2)

Allow me to be Your heart for someone in distress, Savior.

The American Nurse

Carolyn Jones' interest in nurses began after she was diagnosed with breast cancer years ago. As she began intense chemotherapy treatments, she was cared for by a nurse named Joanne Staha, whose positive way of dealing with patients made a tremendous difference to Jones' mind and spirit.

That experience set the filmmaker on a journey to explore the lives of these quiet, unknown healers all around the country. The result was a Christopher Award-winning documentary called *The American Nurse*, which profiles five nurses in vastly different settings as they deal with miscarriage, aging, war, poverty, and prison life.

Though it sounds like a cliché, the love and kindness these nurses show their patients has a life-changing effect on them. During a *Christopher Closeup* interview, Jones admitted, "Ever since I've done all of this work with nurses, I actually speak in those clichés now. I wish they weren't clichés...but they're true! Kindness and love can change so much."

Your wounds I will heal. (Jeremiah 30:17)

Help me appreciate the vital role that compassionate, talented nurses bring to the world, Divine Healer.

Remembering Mom

Christian poet Sheila Gosney wrote a Mother's Day poem for people who have lost their moms. Here is an excerpt:

"Mother's Day is special for the expressions of gratitude and honor you can give to your mother...But the holiday is bittersweet...when you've lost your mother and she's not around. While other people choose flowers and cards of endearment, your tears softly slip to the ground. For you know that your mother was simply like no other for she was one-in-a-million to you. And you know she made sacrifices...putting her needs aside for the tasks that she needed to do.

"When you close your eyes, you picture her face and all the phrases you can still hear her say. You remember her faith and how she shared it with you when she clung to the Word and she prayed. You look at the person you turned out to be and you're grateful your mother was true. For all the lessons she taught and the love she instilled are now woven into all that you do. Though you can't buy her flowers on Mother's Day, memories linger of when she was here. You honor her life by giving the blessings to others that she gave you every day of the year."

Be comforted for your grief. (Sirach 38:17)

Bless the souls of all mothers in Thy care, Father.

Raising a Gentleman

When Aljelani "AJ" Igwe graduated from LEAP Academy University Charter School in Camden, New Jersey, his mother, Ovella O'Neal, was so proud of him that she wanted to hire a skywriter to tell the world. But since skywriting disappears too quickly, she paid for a billboard instead.

As reported by *ABC News*, the billboard, which included AJ's graduation picture, read, "A Mother Can't Raise a Man, but I Raised a Gentleman. We Have the Total Package."

O'Neal revealed that she had some rules that kept AJ on the right track—rules like no cell phones or girlfriends because "they're just distractions." However, AJ has always been a "super kid." For instance, she once discovered that he wasn't playing basketball at the local Boys & Girls Club, but attending Bible study instead. And when one of his teachers called her to report that AJ was being a little disrespectful of female teachers, O'Neal had a talk with him and he shaped up quickly.

AJ will attend Rowan College to pursue a career in engineering. With his mom behind him, he's sure to go far.

**Strength and dignity are her clothing.
(Proverbs 31:25)**

Grant mothers the wisdom to raise good children, Lord.

The Right Amount of Exercise

"Exercise has had a Goldilocks problem," declared Gretchen Reynolds in *The New York Times,* "with experts debating just how much exercise is too little, too much or just the right amount to improve health and longevity." However, a new study published in *JAMA Internal Medicine* may finally have found the correct prescription.

In the past, government health guidelines have suggested that people should engage in 150 minutes of moderate exercise per week, which can include something as simple as walking. The study shows the benefits of that approach, demonstrating that those who followed it enjoyed better health and had a "31 percent less risk of dying" than those who did no exercise.

Tripling that amount to 450 minutes a week, however, brought the greatest benefit. "Those people were 39 percent less likely to die prematurely."

So now that you've got the facts, finish reading this reflection—then, get moving!

Do you not know that your body is a temple of the Holy Spirit? (1 Corinthians 6:19)

Motivate me to take good care of my health, Creator.

Stop Helping People?

A pastor in Kansas was organizing an outreach program to demonstrate Christ's love to the community. He phoned several local grocery stores and laundromats for permission to do specific services.

During one call, the employee who answered the phone hesitated, then said, "I'll need to ask the manager, but first, let me make sure I understand: You want to clean up the parking lots, retrieve shopping carts, hold umbrellas for customers, and you don't want anything in return."

"Yes, that's right," said the pastor.

The employee put him on hold. He then came back and said to the pastor, "I'm sorry. We can't let you do that because if we let you do it, we'd have to let everyone else do it, too!"

Imagine if we had to beg people to *stop* helping each other! Chances are that won't happen anytime soon, so in the meantime, keep adding kindness to the world.

The righteous will shine like the sun in the kingdom of their Father. Let anyone with ears listen! (Matthew 13:43)

Teach us how to help each other, Jesus.

Finding Her Way

Two years ago, Liz Gildea was the victim of a sexual assault. At first, she felt justifiably scared and distant, especially from God. Now 21, Gildea has since found renewed hope in the revitalization of her Catholic faith, as well as the devoted companionship of her rescue dog, Jax.

Furthermore, Gildea is eagerly anticipating the second annual "Finding Her Way" retreat, designed for women who, like herself, have been victims of rape. In fact, it was her campaigning to the Diocese of Providence, Rhode Island, that led to the ultimate creation of "Finding Her Way."

The retreat is mainly centered on spiritual healing. Gildea told the *Rhode Island Catholic*, "It's very emotional to be both working on it and attending it as a participant."

She concluded, "My faith is a huge part of my life, and I feel I owe it to myself and others to speak up, and be dynamic in my faith...Maybe in the future we can have some more resources for male survivors as well, or have some female-led support groups in the parishes."

I am your God; I will strengthen you. (Isaiah 41:10)

God, in times of trouble, may we lean upon Your strength.

The First Time Anyone Accomplished This

In May of 2015, Erik Weber became the first student with autism to ever graduate from California Western School of Law. In the same month, he learned that he had passed the bar exam on his first try. His mother, Sandi Weber, told *NBC News*, "It's the first time that anyone that I know of with autism has accomplished this."

When Erik was only five years old, doctors told Sandi that her son should be institutionalized for the rest of his life, but she refused to accept that and devoted her life to working with educators to help him learn in ways that best suited his needs.

She utilized visual learning techniques, enrolled him in the Special Olympics, and once took him campaigning door-to-door to help him learn about facial recognition and the concept of first impressions. Recalling his reaction to learning he had passed the bar, Erik said, "My keyboard got wet with tears of joy."

Today, he practices special education law. Of that calling, he says, "I got into it because I wanted to help other people with special needs, other people like me."

**Blessed is the man who perseveres.
(James 1:12)**

Lord, guide us to seek the good through the trials of life.

Glen Campbell's Courageous Journey

Music legend Glen Campbell, known for hits like *Rhinestone Cowboy* and *Gentle on My Mind*, went on a Goodbye Tour in 2011 not long after learning he had Alzheimer's, a progressive disease that robs people of memory and more.

Campbell and his wife Kim decided to share the story of their current challenges with the singer's audience. In an AARP interview, Kim said, "We wanted to be upfront so that if there were any awkward moments on stage, people would attribute it to the disease and not speculate" since Glen had overcome problems with alcoholism decades earlier.

The three-week tour grew into 151 sold-out shows and inspired a documentary *Glen Campbell... I'll Be Me*. "Offstage, we were struggling," said Kim. But when he sang Glen changed, almost miraculously. "Music is healing."

The Campbells embarked on their tour to help educate and raise awareness. In the process, their courage inspired others on their own challenging life journeys.

Be gracious to me, O Lord, for I am in distress. (Psalm 31:9)

Father, bless all victims of Alzheimer's and dementia, and strengthen the loved ones who care for them.

The Sunny Legacy of Ernie Banks

You don't have to be a Chicago Cubs fan to appreciate the impact Ernie Banks had on baseball. He played for the Cubs, true—a perennially losing team. But you'd never know it from his outlook, which went from sunny to sunnier. When he uttered his mantra, "Let's play two!"—well, darned if he didn't mean it!

Ernie Banks can give all of us a lesson in living. Raised poor in a family of 12 children, he took up baseball in high school and never looked back. As the first black player on the Cubs, he was sometimes criticized for not taking a more active role in civil rights. He had this reply for his critics:

"I care deeply about my people, but I'm not one to go about screaming over what I contribute. I'm not black or white. I'm just a human being trying to survive the only way I know how."

Banks died last year at 83 after a lifetime of making people happy. What a way to live—and what a way to be!

Let no evil talk come out of your mouths, but only what is useful for building up, as there is need, so that your words may give grace to those who hear. (Ephesians 4:29)

May the joy in my heart radiate Your joy to others, Father.

Jesus Loves Families

Father Bill Byrne's words of wisdom in the *Catholic Standard*, newspaper of the Archdiocese of Washington, D.C., once outlined "five ways that Jesus loves families."

- **Bethlehem and Nazareth.** "Born of Mary, taught by Joseph to be a good man, this is how Jesus came to save us."

- **Cana.** "When Jesus performed His first miracle at a wedding, it's clear He expected great things from husbands and wives."

- **Bridegroom.** "Jesus described Himself as a bridegroom...the family is one [way] the Church builds up the Kingdom of God."

- **Behold Your Mother.** "Jesus loves families so much that He made his whole Church one great family of love."

- **Sacrament of Love.** "He raised marriage to the level of a sacrament so that it would be a visible sign to make present His love to all humanity."

If people ever ask what makes your family different, he concludes, "Tell them with a smile, 'It's Jesus Christ! He loves families, you know!'"

**You shall be My sons and daughters.
(2 Corinthians 6:18)**

Help me love all members of our human family, Lord.

An Ebola Patient's Faith

When 26-year-old nurse Nina Pham treated an Ebola patient at Texas Health Presbyterian Hospital: Dallas in 2014, she wound up contracting the potentially fatal disease herself.

During her treatment, she released this message: "I'm doing well and want to thank everyone for their kind wishes and prayers. I am blessed by the support of family and friends and am blessed to be cared for by the best team of doctors and nurses in the world."

Faith and blessings didn't just become part of Pham's life when she was fighting for survival. Tom Ha, who knows Pham since she was in eighth grade, told *CNN*, "She is a very devoted Catholic, and always puts other people's interests ahead of her own. She comes from a family that is [of] a very strong faith...I think that she takes [nursing] as more than a career. I think it's a vocation, because her family, from the time that we met, they always serve other people."

Thankfully, Pham survived and can continue in her vocation of serving others through nursing.

Restore me to health and make me live. (Isaiah 38:16)

May illness not shake our faith, Divine Healer.

Mastering 'Soft Skills'

"Work ethic" is a favorite topic of Mike Rowe, who hosts TV series like *Dirty Jobs* and *Somebody's Gotta Do It* about necessary-but-often-overlooked types of manual labor. He also champions jobs like "plumber" and "electrician" because there's actually a shortage of them in the United States.

On Facebook, Rowe shared an experience which feeds into his belief that there is an adversity to hard work in today's world: "I talked to several hiring managers from a few of the largest companies in Michigan. They all told me the same thing—the biggest under-reported challenge in finding good help is an overwhelming lack of 'soft skills.' That's a polite way of saying that many applicants don't tuck their shirts in, or pull their pants up, or look you in the eye, or say things like 'please' and 'thank you.' This is not a Michigan problem—this is a national crisis."

The soft skills Rowe talks about aren't difficult to master, yet they can make a tremendous difference in social and business relationships. Practice them yourself and you'll be teaching others by example.

In all toil there is profit. (Proverbs 14:23)

Remind us of the importance of simple manners, Lord.

Life is Precious

Most people have no troubling thoughts about suicide. In general, it's the furthest thing from their minds. That's not true, though, with some young women. And it's particularly the case with young Latina adolescents.

According to statistics from the Centers for Disease Control, the number of Latina teens who have seriously considered suicide has risen alarmingly in recent years, where it stands at 13.3 percent in New York—more than double the rate for white American girls.

Albor Ruiz pointed to the problems in his *Daily News* column, citing the work of Rosa Maria Gil. She founded Life Is Precious, a suicide prevention program for Latinas in New York, which recently opened its third center in the city.

Culture shock is behind much of the problem, and Life Is Precious teaches young women to develop the skills they need to combat it, while also helping them discover new talents.

"There is no other place doing this kind of work for Latina teens in this country," Gil said. "There is so much need."

The prayer of faith will save the sick. (James 5:15)

Guide those who see no hope toward a lifeline, Savior. Help them to choose life.

The Wisdom of Yogi

Is there anyone who doesn't appreciate a good Yogi Berra story? The *Daily News* of New York didn't think so, so it dispatched several reporters to collect comments and quotes from various people in the baseball world about Yogi at the time of his 90th birthday last year.

These days Berra lives in a retirement community in West Caldwell, New Jersey, and appreciated all the stories—most of which ended with the thought that Yogi Berra is the nicest guy in the world, which is quite a great way to be thought of.

One of the best stories came via Yogi's lifelong buddy, Joe Garagiola, also a catcher of note, who grew up near him in St. Louis. Garagiola and Berra visited each other on Thanksgivings, and one year Joe, driving from Westchester County in New York, got lost on the way to Yogi's New Jersey home. He called in desperation from a phone booth on the Garden State Parkway. "Hey Yog, we're lost," he said. "You've got to help us."

"Okay," replied Berra, ever accommodating. "Where are you?"

Our mouth was filled with laughter.
(Psalm 126:2)

Send me friends who make me laugh, Heavenly Father.

A Hike the Marines Will Never Forget

For a company of Marines training at Camp Lejeune, North Carolina, the only unusual thing about their hike one day last year—Feb. 19, to be exact—was the extreme cold. It was frigid, all right, but everything else about the hike—the field pack, the 10-mile march—was strictly routine.

They'd completed about six of those miles when, up ahead, they spotted a parked car with its hazard lights flashing. In a moment, someone was yelling something that made everybody stop: a woman inside the car was having a baby!

The Marines remained calm under pressure and took control of the situation. As soon as the baby was born, a corpsman tied its umbilical cord, then wrapped the mother and baby as warmly as possible to protect them from the bitter cold. Someone had already called an ambulance, and when it arrived, the paramedics helped get the family inside it quickly.

No more than 10 minutes after the emergency began, it was over, and the Marines resumed their march. "You always see that in movies," said one hiker. "Now I can say I've done it too."

**I will cry out like a woman in labor.
(Isaiah 42:14)**

Lord, protect and strengthen all expectant mothers.

Church Groundskeeper Replaced by Sheep

The groundskeeper at Old St. Patrick's Cathedral cemetery in downtown Manhattan told the pastor, Monsignor Sakano, that he was thinking about retiring. How, he wondered, would the priest tend to the grass and bushes when that came to pass?

"I'll get sheep," responded Msgr. Sakano. And so he did.

As reported by *Eyewitness News*, the sheep are rented from an upstate farm whenever the grounds need some work. When they first arrived at the church, the grass was 10 inches high.

In addition to meeting a practical need, the three sociable ewes—named Mulberry, Elizabeth, and Mott after the streets that border the church—are also popular with parishioners and neighbors. The local locksmith even alarmed their pen and put in cameras so they can be monitored.

Another benefit: the sheep are more environmentally friendly than a gas-powered mower, making Msgr. Sakano's creative solution a win-win for church and community.

Know that the Lord is God. It is He that made us, and we are His; we are His people, and the sheep of His pasture. (Psalm 100:3)

May we appreciate the blessing of animals, Creator.

Why is Dad So Mad?

What do you do when you've got a problem that's hitting your own home, your own family? If you're Seth Kastle, you write a book about it, and you hope it will help to improve things. In Kastle's case, that's just what happened.

Seth Kastle of Wakeeney, Kansas, is an Army veteran who's been deployed to Afghanistan and Iraq. As a result of his service there, he came home to his wife and daughters with post-traumatic stress disorder—PTSD. "I struggle with anger," Kastle said. "That's probably my main symptom. I also have some issues that go with my memory."

Kastle's book, called *Why Is Dad So Mad?*, was self-published after a fund-raising campaign—and after attempts to explain his problems to his children met with only partial success. After reading the book they felt differently. "No matter what," said Kastle's daughter, age six, "when they're mad or sad at you, they still love you."

Kastle hopes other military families will explain PTSD to their kids. "It's not always going to be easy," he said. "but they'll get through it."

They have fled...from the stress of battle. (Isaiah 21:15)

Bless our military with the care they need, Divine Healer.

Teen Goes to Bat for Those in Need

Lexi Serek had an idea. She enjoyed the good things in life, while others did not. Why not do what she could to make things a bit easier for them? Her options were admittedly limited.

Last year she was a junior at DePaul Catholic High School, in Wayne, New Jersey, where, among other things, she was a utility player on the softball team. What she decided was this: she would collect used softball equipment, clean and repair it if necessary, and donate it to teams which had no equipment at all.

With the help of her Dad, working through a league in Montville, she scored big time. As Lexi told Darren Cooper of *The Record*, she collected 100 gloves, 100 bats, 250 softballs, 60 helmets and 50 uniforms—all in good shape. She found a ready recipient at a center in Camden, and off she went to deliver them—in person.

"I realize how lucky I am," she said. "I know there are places where parents aren't trying to figure out how to buy a new bat; they're thinking about putting food on the table. So I thought this would be a good idea."

**Open your hand to the poor.
(Deuteronomy 15:11)**

Help young people learn positive values from sports, Lord.

Keep Watch, Dear Lord

Most of us are used to speaking to God in our own words. But at times, traditional prayers, including prayers from other faiths or backgrounds, can enhance our reflections.

Rev. William Kolb of Calvary Episcopal Church in Memphis has a special feeling for this ancient prayer which is said at the end of the day. He finds in it a reminder that "Ours is a God of compassion for 'all sorts and conditions' of humankind...And we need God to help us remain sensitively and caringly aware of the suffering of others."

Here then is the beautiful prayer: "Keep watch, dear Lord, with those who work, or watch, or weep this night, and give Thine angels charge over those who sleep. Tend the sick, Lord Christ; give rest to the weary, bless the dying, soothe the suffering, pity the afflicted, shield the joyous; and all for Thy love's sake. Amen."

Come, bless the Lord, all you servants of the Lord, who stand by night in the house of the Lord. (Psalm 134:1)

Christ, be our shelter and lamp during the hours of darkness.

Remembering the Doughboys

Since Memorial Day 1923, a bronze statue of an American soldier has stood in Doughboy Park in the Woodside section of Queens, New York. It was put there as a tribute to those who died fighting in World War I, but has come to represent more.

Korean War veteran Ed Bergendahl, age 82, spends hours in the park educating visitors about the monument and surrounding memorial gardens. He told Rich Schapiro of the *Daily News* that the word "doughboy" was "the nickname British soldiers gave American GIs in the first World War—a nod to the over-sized round buttons on the American uniforms that reminded the Brits of the doughboy cakes so popular at home."

The park has evolved into a memorial for others as well. A plaque includes the names of first responders killed on 9/11—and a "Heroes Garden" serves as a tribute to members of the military killed in Iraq and Afghanistan and the four Americans murdered at the U.S. Embassy in Benghazi, Libya, in 2012.

Bergendahl concludes, "They're all heroes."

The memory of the righteous is a blessing. (Proverbs 10:7)

May we never forget those who died for our country, Lord.

Gunboat Judy

From the moment they met, Frank and Judy became the best of friends. The time was 1941, the place a Japanese prison camp. Frank Williams was a captured English officer, and Judy was the dog he befriended—a pointer, weakened terribly by near-starvation. Williams shared his meager ration of rice with her, and a fast friendship was born.

Judy helped keep up Williams' spirits and those of his fellow captives, especially when they were crammed into the hold of one of Japan's infamous prison ships. When the ship was attacked by British torpedoes, Williams forced Judy through a porthole to safety and later jumped from the deck himself. They didn't see each other for two days—and then were reunited when an overjoyed Judy playfully knocked Williams to the ground in a prison camp along the Singapore River.

When the war ended, the dog was held up in England by a six-month quarantine. By this time, though, she had become a tabloid heroine, nicknamed "Gunboat Judy." And when she was released from quarantine, she was honored as a military hero.

Who teaches us more than the animals? (Job 35:11)

Bless man's best friend with kind owners, Prince of Peace.

Music Draws Kids Out of Themselves

Adam Goldberg thinks that music can change the lives of disabled children—and he's been doing just that, as a New York City public school teacher, for 21 years. What's more, he believes that the power of song can draw kids out of themselves and into the world, even when nothing else has worked.

"Give them a mike and they'll start singing, even if they're silent the rest of the time," Goldberg told Ben Chapman of the *Daily News* after being nominated for the paper's Hometown Hero Award. "You can see the confidence level starting to build as soon as they start to play."

A one-time jazz musician, Goldberg, 53, uses traditional instruments such as keyboards and drums to reach students with disabilities that range from autism to cerebral palsy. Singing, he said, helps with speech issues, and playing in a band can help those with anxiety become more comfortable working with others. "They feel the power of community and teamwork," he said. "It's all part of this wonderful thing we're doing together."

Praise the Lord with the lyre. (Psalm 33:2)

Divine Healer, may the harmony of music establish feelings of harmony within each of us.

Two Weddings, 20 Years Apart

Briggs Fussy and Brittney Husbyn walked down the aisle together at age three. At the time, of course, he was the ring-bearer and she was the flower girl in somebody else's wedding. Twenty years later, they walked down the aisle again—this time as husband and wife.

Neither of them remembered many details about the long-ago wedding, but both their mothers kept a picture of the pair hanging in their homes. Briggs' unique name stuck in Brittney's mind so when she heard her ninth-grade teacher mention a new transfer student with the same name, she knew it had to be her old wedding partner.

The couple didn't start dating until their junior year of high school, and endured a long-distance relationship when they attended different colleges. But Briggs eventually returned to their home state of Minnesota so they could be together for good.

Brittney told *CNN*, "It's all a part of God's plan. All fate for sure."

Clothe yourselves with love, which binds everything together in perfect harmony. (Colossians 3:14)

May husbands and wives cherish each other, Lord.

A Wartime Act of Courage

The 13th-century Church of St. Denis in Remy, a village northeast of Paris, France, had been missing its stained-glass windows for over 50 years. During World War II, the U.S. Army attacked a German train stopped near the village. That train was full of munitions and blew up. An American lieutenant was killed in the explosion, and the church's windows blew out.

Villagers, at great risk to their own lives, took the lieutenant's body from the wreckage and kept it hidden until they could give the young man a proper burial in the local cemetery. When American troops liberated Remy, the villagers showed them the lieutenant's grave.

The villagers' act of courage led to an act of charity. In 1996, the men of U.S. Army Air Corps 364th Fighter Group, in which the lieutenant had served, started collecting the $200,000 needed to restore the church's windows.

By July 2000, the windows were installed. A grateful village welcomed several veterans from the 364th to the window dedication, and celebrated their long-ago contribution to the world's fight for freedom.

May the Lord reward you for your deeds. (Ruth 2:12)

May acts of courage never be forgotten, Savior.

A Christopher Prayer for Memorial Day

Heavenly Father, today we honor those who gave their lives for their country on foreign battlefields and here at home. Though they would have preferred peace to war, they responded to the call to serve and made the ultimate sacrifice defending the ideals in which they believed, and defending innocents from violence. May their souls be embraced by You.

We pray for those service members whose invisible wounds led them to take their own lives. Their minds and spirits were in turmoil due to the violence they had experienced, and they thought there was no other way to end their pain. Welcome these men and women into Your loving and merciful heart. We also pray that those enduring these struggles right now realize that suicide is not the answer.

Finally, comfort the families of all the men and women who have been lost to war and terrorism. Help these families remember the good times, and look forward to being reunited with their loved ones in Your heavenly kingdom someday where there will be no more mourning. Amen.

No one has greater love than this, to lay down one's life for one's friends. (John 15:13)

Send Your grace to all military families, Prince of Peace.

Heart's Home

The best neighbors you could ever find are living in a slum. They'll pick you up when your car breaks down or drive you to the hospital if you get sick in the middle of the night. Who exactly are these neighbors? They're volunteers for the ministry Heart's Home, which works in 21 countries worldwide.

In an interview with *Catholic Digest*, volunteer Natalia Fassano explained that Heart's Home began 25 years ago to offer "young people, ages 18 to 32, a strong experience of prayer, service to the poor, and community life." Six or seven people live in a house in the chosen community and reach out to those who are suffering or living in poverty.

Fassano's latest assignment is Brooklyn, New York, because "the poverty of New York is a tremendous cry of loneliness," especially from the elderly and homeless women with psychological problems. She concludes, "We want to be the presence of Christ among them."

Turn to me and be gracious to me, for I am lonely and afflicted. (Psalm 25:16)

Increase the compassion in my heart, Divine Healer, so that I can offer shelter to the suffering and lonely.

Rickey and Robinson

The late baseball executive Branch Rickey made his place in history by signing Jackie Robinson to a major-league baseball contract over 60 years ago, breaking the "color line" that had excluded African-Americans from the game.

Rickey initially professed no great interest in social justice: "I simply wanted to win a pennant for the Brooklyn Dodgers, and I wanted the best human beings I could find to help me win it."

As he and Robinson grew closer, Rickey gave more attention to the race issue. This conservative midwestern Methodist pressed for government action on civil rights. Later, Rickey would say his initial reason for hiring Robinson was "good and sufficient. However...it wasn't the whole truth."

Still, Rickey not only did the right thing, he was open to learning and evolving as a human being. And the residue of his design benefitted not just a sport, but a country.

There is no longer Jew or Greek...all of you are one in Christ Jesus. (Galatians 3:28)

Father of All, may we not judge others by appearances, but rather by the goodness of their actions.

An Idol's Kindness

Anorexia and bipolar disorder had left twenty-something college student Jill in a dark place that kept getting darker. That started changing when she saw singer Brooke White on season seven of *American Idol.*

One night, White sang the Beatles' classic *Let It Be*, which includes the lyric, "When I find myself in times of trouble, Mother Mary comes to me, speaking words of wisdom, let it be."

On her blog, Jill recalled how that performance spoke to her heart with its message of hope. She resolved to meet White at one of the Idol summer concerts and write her a letter that explained her struggles and the meaning of her performance.

Jill got tickets to several Idol concerts, briefly met White at one of them, and handed her the letter. At another show two days later, White came looking for Jill, talked with her at length, and helped get her into treatment. Jill wrote, "She was quick not to take any credit...She always turned it back to God and needing to do it hand-in-hand with Him. That's when I knew without a doubt she was the real deal."

Let us...provoke one another to love and good deeds. (Hebrews 10:24)

Help me take the opportunity to practice kindness, Father.

A Lesson in Self-Esteem

Popular television preacher Joel Osteen once opened his sermon with the following joke:

There was a kindergarten teacher, who wanted to teach her students about self-esteem. She said to her class, "Everyone who thinks you are dumb, please stand up."

The teacher didn't think anybody would stand, which would allow her to make her point that no one was dumb. But about that time little Jonny stood up, so she didn't quite know what to do.

She said, "Now Jonny, do you really think that you're dumb?"

He said "No Ma'am, I just hate to see you standing there all by yourself."

While Osteen's joke is funny, it's also a good reminder to treat others with Jonny's level of empathy and compassion.

As God's chosen ones, holy and beloved, clothe yourselves with compassion, kindness, humility, meekness, and patience. (Colossians 3:12)

May I always embrace a sense of humor, Father.

Achieving a Work/Life Balance

Chicago-based professional counselor Julia Hogan knows that it can be difficult to achieve a good work/life balance, so she offered several suggestions on *Verily* magazine's website:

- **Set Work Boundaries and Stick to Them.** "Always being 'on call' is a big contributor to work-related stress because you never truly stop working. Decide how and when you will be reachable after office hours...Always being on call can lead to burnout."

- **Take Your Paid Time Off.** "Seventy-five percent of American workers don't use all their paid vacation days...Entrepreneur Seth Bannon explains the problem with not taking those hard-earned vacation days: 'Professional runners take long breaks between marathons. They make no excuses for this, and no one judges them for it, because everyone knows that rest and recuperation is an essential part of being a pro athlete. The same is true for entrepreneurs (and everyone, really)...It's time we stopped making excuses for rest and relaxation.'"

Come away to a deserted place all by yourselves and rest a while. (Mark 6:31)

Lord, I am grateful for my job, but it can be overwhelming at times. Guide me toward moments of rest and peace.

Who Are the Best Role Models?

When Tim Shriver was in his 20s and 30s, he felt confused about his place in the world. Where, he wondered, could he find role models that would help him incorporate his faith into his career? As a member of the famed Kennedy family, he had access to the best people the world had to offer—celebrities, Nobel Prize Winners, CEOs, politicians—but they all fell short.

As Shriver explained during a *Christopher Closeup* interview about his book *Fully Alive*, "I found [answers]...in the insights of centering prayer, in the great and long tradition in Christianity." This helped him look at the intellectually challenged young people his parents helped through Special Olympics with new eyes.

He said, "I could see more clearly the gifts of my fellow human beings, who often were seen by the culture as being disabled or deformed or invalid, and I began to have great moments of fulfillment and happiness in their presence."

He leads the humble in what is right, and teaches the humble His way. (Psalm 25:9)

Don't let me be fooled by the trappings of riches and fame, Lord. Your truth and beauty lie within the humble.

The Man Who Loved Money

A man who loved money was so consumed with making it and having it, that he could hardly see the sense in anything beyond its relationship to the almighty dollar.

Once, after a sermon, he decided to argue some points of it that he did not understand. The preacher, realizing where the difficulty lay, opened the Bible and pointed to the word "God."

"Can you see that?"

"Of course I can," replied the man indignantly.

The preacher then took a coin from his pocket and placed it over the word and asked, "Can you see it now?"

"Of course not. How can I see it through a coin?"

"Exactly," replied the preacher.

There may be things that blur our ability to see our lives clearly. Becoming absorbed with any one idea may obscure other aspects of our lives that are beautiful as well as important. Consider whether there's anything in your life that blurs your vision.

Guard against all kinds of greed. (Luke 12:15)

I yearn to see You more clearly, Lord.

From Victim to Victor

In March, 2013, 20-year-old Maya Leggat was waiting at the White Plains station of MetroNorth in New York when a stranger crept up behind her and pushed her in front of an oncoming train. She suffered two broken legs and a severed finger in the incident, and endured months of surgeries and rehabilitation. But last May, Leggat graduated from Hunter College with a 3.8 grade point average and special honors in English. And the three police officers who heroically rescued her were there, with her parents, to pay her tribute.

"She was the toughest person I've ever seen in my life under circumstances like that," said one of them. With blood gushing from her leg that day, she remained conscious. "I know I'm badly hurt," she said. "Just do what you need to do."

Leggat kept up her lessons while recuperating, reading textbooks from her hospital bed and following classroom discussions via Skype. At the graduation, she reflected on her fate to the *Daily News's* Rich Schapiro: "How lucky I am to be here today with people I love and people who care about me."

With God we shall do valiantly. (Psalm 108:13)

Abba, sustain me through life's trials.

Cop Leads Survivors to Safety

When Amtrak Train 188 derailed last year in Philadelphia, killing eight people and injuring some 200, many people aboard played heroic roles. One of them was Police Officer Michael Keane of Lyndhurst, New Jersey, who ignored his own injuries and led two carloads of passengers to safety before local police took over.

Keane was sitting with his fiancée, Courtney Keegan of nearby North Arlington, when the deadly accident occurred. They were in the last car of the Washington-New York train, five rows from the end. After making sure his fiancée had no serious injuries, he exited the car by the rear door to check the terrain. He then led Keegan and nearby passengers out the same way

Keane returned to the train and, using a conductor's flashlight, led the remaining passengers in his car, and the next car forward, to safety. "I'm a police officer," he called out. "The door's open back here. Follow the light and follow me out."

He described his feelings to Stefanie Dazio of the Hackensack *Record*. "You click into another mode," he said. "I just went to work. That's all it comes down to."

Be ready for every good work. (Titus 3:1)

Guide our leadership efforts always, Holy Spirit.

Leaving a Spiritual Will

Rabbi Moses Yehosua Zelig Hakohen, a religious leader in Latvia in the 1800s, redefined the meaning of a "will" when he wrote a spiritual will, leaving these bits of spiritual wealth to his children and grandchildren:

- Prepare yourself in the morning to serve the Creator and pray with utmost devotion.

- Train yourself in the habit of balance, expecting equal amounts of criticism and praise, sadness and joy, pain and pleasure.

- Avoid listening to any obscene speech.

- Trust that God will do everything for your benefit.

Our legacy to those we leave behind should not be measured in bank accounts. Gifts of the Spirit and the heart are worth far more.

Yours, O Lord, are the greatness, the power, the glory, the victory, and the majesty. (1 Chronicles 29:11)

Spirit of Life and Love, guide my actions today and every day.

Aaron Neville's Spiritual Roots

Singer Aaron Neville is, rather famously, a New Orleans native, so it was fitting that Peter Finney Jr., editor of the New Orleans *Clarion-Herald*, told his life story in a column last year.

He reported that Neville, then 74, was about to receive the University of Notre Dame's Laetare Medal, which celebrates "genius [that] has ennobled the arts and sciences," and that illustrates the ideals of the church. Neville recalled the time he had painfully crawled on his knees up the steps of the Shrine of St. Ann in the Crescent City, along with how his mother had taught him about St. Jude, the patron of lost causes.

Neville is abundantly familiar with lost causes, having been through many in his lifetime. But he had even more highlights that stem from his Catholic roots. "I always could feel there was a light at the end of the tunnel because St. Monica School gave me a lot of morals, something that's sunk in me that is still inside me," Neville told Finney. And on every album he records, Neville makes sure there's a spiritual track, something like *The Lord's Prayer*. That's one way he has of saying, "Thank You."

Let us sing to the Lord. (Psalm 95:1)

Keep me grounded in the roots of my faith, King of Kings.

The Smile of God

Since God is pure spirit, we can't actually see Him smile. Or can we? In his book *God Delights in You*, Father John Catoir, the former Director of The Christophers, recalled a vacation in Ontario when he sat on the bank of the Madawaska River next to 89-year-old Tom Mahon.

Surrounded by his grandchildren and great-grandchildren, wrote Father Catoir, "[Mahon's] smile was a perfect expression of God's radiant satisfaction with His children. If you think about it, the smile of God is more visible than you might think. We can see it reflected in the noble sentiments of our brothers and sisters everywhere. What's even more exciting, we can evoke it by loving one another.

"Being made in God's image, we not only belong to Him, we can reflect Him, we can think like Him, and we can love the way He loves: selflessly and unconditionally. In this relationship with God, we are able to offer ourselves to Him and become channels of His mercy...Nothing could be more personal."

A glad heart makes a cheerful countenance. (Proverbs 15:13)

Inspire me to smile and reflect Your love, Divine Creator.

Courage on the Court

When Desiree Andrews, a cheerleader with Down Syndrome at Lincoln Middle School in Kenosha, Wisconsin, was getting bullied from the stands during a game, a few boys from the basketball team took action.

"The kids in the audience were picking on Dee, so we all stepped forward," one of the players told *TMJ4*, a local news station. "It's not fair when other people get treated wrong," another told *Kenosha News*, "because we're all the same. We're all created the same way. God made us the same way."

Reporting on the story, *BuzzFeed* featured a photo of team members walking hand in hand with Desiree through the school, with a caption that read, "Now Desiree, who they call Dee, never walks to class alone."

The gym has been affectionately renamed "Dee's House," and the team played the final game in her honor, with the boys chanting, "Whose house? Dee's House!" Desiree called her friends' gesture "sweet, kind, awesome, amazing."

Do not be frightened or dismayed, for the Lord your God is with you wherever you go. (Joshua 1:9)

Lord, strengthen us to defend the dignity of all Your children.

Disagreeable Teen, Disagreeable Adult?

Most parents deal with disagreeable teenagers, but a study out of the University of Virginia reveals that some young people aren't growing out of that phase.

Researchers followed 164 adolescents over 10 years and discovered that those who were especially rude, argumentative, and saw only their own points of view as worthy of respect suffered from problematic relationships when they got older—though they weren't actually aware of this fact. While the study subjects thought their relationships were fine, their friends or partners noted they were often impossible to get along with.

Lead researcher Christopher Hafen told the *Chicago Tribune's* Heidi Stevens that this problem is called "relationship blindness," and parents should be aware of it so they can try to counteract it by engaging teens in conversation about big issues and getting them to look beyond their own opinions. And most importantly, parents should model agreeable behavior themselves. Teens will emulate what they see at home.

Set the believers an example in speech and conduct. (1 Timothy 4:12)

Inspire adults to be role models for teenagers, Lord.

Amazing Grace

The Christopher News Note "Opening Yourself to God's Grace" includes the often-told story of John Newton, a 19th-century sailor who became a minister. If it's unfamiliar territory to you, you're in for a treat; if you've seen it before, it's well worth looking at again.

John Newton was a ship's captain, known as "The Great Blasphemer" for the coarseness of his language. He was a slave trader, giving little quarter to anyone. One night his ship was buffeted by high winds during a terrible storm, and he found himself turning to God for help. The ship was saved, and Newton wrote that the Lord "delivered me out of deep waters." The event changed his life. He gave up his seafaring ways, ultimately became a minister, and even denounced the slave trade.

And he wrote hymns. They were sung by his congregation, and one of them has endured to this day. Its words will surely be familiar to you. It goes like this: "Amazing grace! How sweet the sound that saved a wretch like me. I once was lost but now am found, was blind but now I see."

By grace you have been saved through faith. (Ephesians 2:8)

Infuse my heart with Your grace, Holy Spirit.

Cop Opens Home and Heart to Brothers

Josh and Jessee were brothers who had been bounced around from foster home to foster home, enduring poverty and hardship. The highlight of their week was training at Pittsburgh's Steel City Boxing Gym, a nonprofit where children could not only work out, but also receive some much-needed mentoring.

That's where 45-year-old bachelor Detective Jack Mook took the two boys under his wing. Josh was only nine years old when the detective became his personal trainer. This was the beginning of a six-year bond that would lead Mook to his most challenging but rewarding vocation yet: fatherhood.

When Detective Mook learned the dire extent of the boys' living situation from 15-year-old Josh, he was unwilling to let the boys suffer any longer. He obtained an emergency order to become their foster parent. This past September, Detective Mook officially adopted them. "Since the adoption, you can see that family feeling is coming over us," Mook told *Today's* Lisa Flam. "It means everything. It's a commitment...and it's a good one."

> **Sons are indeed a heritage from the Lord...Happy is the man who has...them. (Psalm 127:4-5)**

Father, bless all parents, and guide them in Your ways.

Awesome Dad Hall of Fame

In 2014, the clothing website Johnnie-O held a contest inviting people to explain why their fathers should be in their "Awesome Dad Hall of Fame." The winning essay came from Mindi Santaniello Craddock. Here is an excerpt:

"My Dad, Paul Santaniello, is a superhero... Throughout my life, my Dad has been a stable, loving presence, supporting and guiding me through my trials, sharing my triumphs, and acting as a role model of how a man should be...

"And when I was faced with the unimaginable: a cancer diagnosis at 35 with three young kids of my own...and he told me everything would be okay and I could beat this...I believed him. Even though it wasn't okay and it was hard, I felt strong by his belief in me, and I felt protected and supported by his love and commitment. And I beat [the cancer].

"The definition of a superhero isn't the guy in a cape with special powers saving humanity from villains and disasters. [It's] a person who is stable and committed and loyal, someone who impacts lives with compassion, kindness, honesty, reliability and love. And guess what? That's SO my Dad!"

With all your heart honor your father. (Sirach 7:27)

Inspire fathers to be models of what a man should be, Lord.

The Content of Their Character

The nine murders that took place at Emanuel A.M.E. Church in Charleston, South Carolina, on June 17, 2015, shocked the country and the world. The fact that they occurred in a house of worship during Bible study just added to the horror.

While everyone mourned for the victims and their families, we should also look at the two divergent worldviews that played a role in the incident. Though the church where the crime took place primarily serves African-Americans, the Bible study group welcomed Dylann Roof, a young white stranger, to join them.

They saw him as a fellow human being made in the image and likeness of God. Roof, however, saw them as an image and likeness he had created in his own mind based on every negative stereotype you can think of. These innocents were essentially martyred because of the color of their skin. The content of their character didn't matter to the killer.

All of us need to pray for the wisdom to see people as people and not as labels. The future of society depends on it.

Just as I have loved you, you also should love one another. (John 13:34)

Holy Spirit, move us past the sin of racism.

Meeting Hate with Prayer and Love

The day after the murder of nine people at Emanuel A.M.E. Church in Charleston, South Carolina, Hallie Lord went to a scheduled appointment at her obstetrician's office for a check-up on her pregnancy. One of the nurses there, she learned, was a member of the church.

Writing on Facebook, Lord said, "It was heartbreaking to witness her grief, which was so young and raw, especially set against the backdrop of growing bellies and new life. I wanted to hug her but I didn't know if she wanted to be hugged so I just sat and said a prayer...I couldn't help but overhear her conversation with one of the other nurses and it took my breath away.

"This beautiful woman wasn't raging (though surely she had the right)...and she didn't seem hopeless (though who could have blamed her). She simply sat gracefully with her grief, told her story, and asked people to pray. And not just to pray but to please, please just keep loving one another."

Prayer and love. If we all did more of those simple things, imagine how much better the world would be.

Pray for one another. (James 5:16)

Help us overcome evil with love, Father.

Dad's Best Advice

For Father's Day 2015, many U.S. Olympians and Paralympians shared the best advice their dads had given them on the Team USA website. Here are a few responses:

- Five-time Paralympic swimming medalist Aimee Bruder: "My parents showed and told me that there is no substitute for hard work. The efforts put in are also done in the shadows. That is, in the early morning to late at night when no one is watching."

- Seven-time Olympic gymnastics medalist Shannon Miller: "At one of my first competitions, I ran over to my dad after two events and asked what score I needed to win. He looked at me...and said 'Shannon, it doesn't matter what the score is. Go out there and try your best during every routine.' I'm not sure I ever looked at another score. Instead I simply gave 100 percent every time out."

- Olympic figure skater Polina Edmunds: "One quote my dad always says in the morning to wake us up is: 'Rise and shine, and give God your glory.'"

Fathers...bring [your children] up in the discipline and instruction of the Lord. (Ephesians 6:4)

Grant our earthly fathers divine wisdom, Holy Spirit.

A Match Made in Heaven

In 2014, Ashley McIntyre from Louisville, Kentucky, offered to donate her kidney to Danny Robinson, whom she had never met. She learned about him from her mother, who heard his story on the radio.

The sadness of Robinson's story was compounded by the fact that his father had died of cancer two years earlier. And the year before that, his house burned down. McIntyre told *ABC News,* "It was like one thing after another for them."

Though it's rare for a living donor's kidney to be a match for a stranger, tests proved McIntyre and Robinson, both age 25, were compatible. Once everything was finalized, their families got together at a local restaurant, where everyone "clicked immediately," especially McIntyre and Robinson.

They started dating after the surgery, and soon got married. In 2015, the couple was expecting to give birth to a baby girl, who will hear an interesting story one day about how her parents met. As McIntyre said, "It was all planned out by God."

It is Your providence, O Father, that steers its course. (Wisdom 14:3)

Lord, grant us the vision to see Your mysterious ways.

A Father's Mission of Suicide Prevention

"I knew our son was sad, but I didn't know he could die from being too sad," recalled retired Major Gen. Mark Graham about his son Kevin's suicide on June 21, 2003.

Kevin was an ROTC cadet who had always been a great student, but feelings of loneliness and depression started getting the better of him. He received counseling and medication, but didn't stick with them, so the downward spiral continued. This was a time before mental health received a lot of attention in the culture. When it was spoken about, there was usually a stigma attached, a stigma that Graham believes led to Kevin's death.

Now, Graham is working to help others before it's too late. For instance, he discovered that suicide is a major problem among college students, so he and his family started a program at the University of Kentucky, where Kevin had attended school, that teaches parents and students about suicide prevention. Warning signs include prolonged feelings of sadness, loneliness even when surrounded by other people, and excessive drinking.

Tomorrow, Graham's efforts to help the military.

O Lord, preserve my life. (Psalm 143:11)

Guide those with depression to the help they need, Lord.

Vet2VetTalk

In light of Major Gen. Graham's long Army career, he is also working to remove the stigma surrounding mental illness and Post-Traumatic Stress Disorder in the military. Specifically, he runs a call center at New Jersey's Rutgers University to give veterans with PTSD the peer support they need.

The program is called Vet2VetTalk, and the phone number is 1-855-838-7481. As Graham said during a *Christopher Closeup* interview, "Veterans can call in 24 hours a day, seven days a week. When the phone rings, a veteran answers and they talk about what they're going through. The callers can talk as long as they want, they can give as little information as they want, it's confidential. It can be anonymous if they choose.

"Our goal is for them to thrive. We work with them to get them into care, whatever they need. Then, when they tell us, 'This has been good, thanks, I appreciate your help,' we tell them, 'Don't forget, you're never alone. You can always call, 24/7, there's a veteran here that'll answer the phone.'"

You have delivered my soul from death. (Psalm 56:13)

Increase my understanding of mental illness, Lord, and make me compassionate toward those who suffer from it.

The Lesson of a Frozen Wedding Cake

Megan Twomey took the remainder of her wedding cake out of the freezer on her first anniversary, but discovered that it had not held up well. Pastry, it seemed, couldn't be frozen to always stay the same.

In an article for *Shalom Tidings* magazine, she then compared that fact to the idea that love can't be frozen to remain the same as it was on your wedding day either—but that isn't a bad thing. Twomey writes, "Love looks different after time, because, love, like people, is meant to grow...We are not meant to be the same people at 40 that we were at 20 or 30.

"As we grow, our perception of love develops. It starts to look less like romantic notes and more like bringing home dinner after a rough day with the kids. It starts to sound less like 'you make me giddy' and more like 'you keep me sane.' It starts to feel less like butterflies in your stomach and more like a strong pillar holding you up. It is not that marriage stops being fun, romantic, or happy. What happens is that...the joy and sorrow you share begin to deepen and steady the love you shared as newlyweds."

Love...endures all things. (1 Corinthians 13:4,7)

Grant couples the maturity to grow in love, Father.

As in Golf, So in Life

The legendary golfer Bobby Jones was a scholar and a teacher as well as a player. Although he quit competitive golf at the age of 28—by which time he had also earned two college degrees and passed the Georgia bar exam—he had won 13 major championships out of the 21 he entered.

Once, Jones wrote, "I never did any real amount of winning until I learned to adjust my ambition." He advised golfers to start every round with these thoughts in mind:

- "I must be prepared for the making of mistakes."
- "I must try always to select the shot to be played and the manner of playing it so as to provide the widest possible margin for error."
- "I must expect to do some scrambling and not be discouraged if the amount of it happens to be more than normal."

As in golf, so in life. Perfection is difficult to come by. Although seldom attained, concentrate on the possibility of it in whatever work is at hand.

Whatever your hand finds to do, do with your might. (Ecclesiastes 9:10)

Though I know I'll never be perfect, may I never double bogey my life's goals, Lord.

Between Children and God

Children talk to God quite naturally—and parents should encourage them. "The home is the most fertile ground for our inner growth," says psychologist Edward Hoffman. "There, each child has the opportunity to gain a strong moral awareness, an appreciation for life and a sense of God's presence in the daily world."

How can parents nurture this budding spirituality? First, use a child's own questions and interests to relate everyday events to our Creator, and emphasize virtues such as charity, justice and courage.

Second, pray with your child. And thirdly, while it may be a truism, actions do speak louder than words. So if you live the kind of meaningful, spiritually rich life you want your youngsters to emulate, they probably will. See the world through a child's eyes and you may gain a clearer vision.

Receive the kingdom of God as a little child. (Mark 10:15)

Father, restore my sense of wonder and clear vision.

An Equine Messenger of Hope

The grueling treatments that Jim Petit endured for his cancer left him feeling exhausted and depressed. His wife Kerry, an animal welfare specialist, wanted to get him out of the house so she took him along to a job in which she was caring for a horse named Diablo.

As reported by Daria Sockey in *Catholic Digest*, "Diablo had been removed from its owner because of neglect and physical abuse. Kerry's job involved daily monitoring the horse at his foster home...to assist in his recovery."

At first, Jim stayed in the car, watching Kerry gently and compassionately teach Diablo that human contact wouldn't bring him pain. As Diablo progressed, Jim's interest in him grew: "He understood what the horse was going through—feeling unwell, powerless, and uncertain of the future....Interest in the horse's recovery gave [Jim] the motivation to maintain a positive attitude about his own. Eventually the Petits adopted Diablo, changing his name to Gabriel. Like his archangel namesake, it seems that Gabriel was sent into their lives by God as a messenger of hope."

Who will see my hope? (Job 17:15)

When all seems lost, Lord, send me a messenger of hope.

Workshop Houston

An award-winning program called Workshop Houston aims at steering youngsters toward college in that city's impoverished Third Ward. But it's not always an easy assignment. Extra-curricular activities are sparse in the ward, and one in four families lives below the poverty line.

That doesn't necessarily daunt the program's co-director, Reginald Hatter. He explained that Workshop Houston, an after-school project, is built around four "shops," three of which are elective: the Beat Shop, in which children learn to make music; the Chopper Shop, where they can modify bikes to look like motorcycles; and the Style Shop, where students design and make clothes. The Scholar Shop, mandatory for attendees, offers homework assistance and lessons on various topics.

Workshop Houston has helped some 1,000 youngsters since it began 12 years ago. And Hatter has big plans for the future. "I would love to have Workshop Dallas, Workshop Los Angeles, Workshop New York," he says. "There's not a doubt in my mind that it's going to happen."

I was a stranger and you welcomed Me. (Matthew 25:35)

Christ, bless and inspire all hardworking students.

Trapped in Stone

Many know about the miners in Chile who were trapped under thousands of feet of rock for more than two months in 2010. Now, journalist Hector Tobar provides exclusive details in his book *Deep Down Dark: The Untold Stories of 33 Men Buried in a Chilean Mine, And the Miracle That Set Them Free.*

Not knowing their fate initially, the miners encouraged one another, and organized regular spiritual discussion sessions as a group. Up top, families kept the faith. Once rescuers made a tiny breakthrough, survival became a possibility and a video link was established with those on the surface.

Tobar wrote that despite being given up for dead because they were "trapped in stone," the video demonstrated "how alive they are, how real and how dirty, looking desperate but sounding hopeful, stuck in a place of darkness and splashing water."

Hope can be a powerful force that sustains us during the most desperate situations. If you feel like you're "trapped in stone," see if you can find some small reason to hold on to hope.

**I cry to You, O Lord; I say, "You are my refuge."
(Psalm 142:5)**

Lord, help us to maintain hope in You when all seems lost.

Until Something Better Comes Along

When Mary Gunning was first hired by Head Start in Baltimore, she told friends she'd hold on to it for a year or so—"until something better comes along." That all happened 33 years ago, and by now it looks like a steady job.

Gunning found herself the guest of honor at the Catholic Charities Annual Dinner in Baltimore last year, accepting a Distinguished Service Award for her years of improving the lives of children and their families through Head Start.

Erik Zygmont reported on the event for the *Catholic Review*, noting that Gunning told the hundreds of guests at the dinner that she'd had opportunities over the years to explore other positions that would have come with a higher salary. "Yet every one of my Charities colleagues in this room tonight," she continued, "knows that's not why we're here."

Gunning not only said she had been inspired by many of the families receiving Head Start services, but she had one other reason she's still on the job 33 years later: "Quite simply, nothing better has come along."

I will instruct you and teach you. (Psalm 32:8)

Guide teachers in their educational mission, Creator.

Just One of the Guys

Jordan Spieth always wanted to win the Masters. Now that he has, what's next?

"Always" might be a little misleading in Spieth's case. He was all of 21 years old when he soared to victory in the major golf tournament last year in Augusta, Georgia, so he's probably got a long way to go.

The sports world has been amazed at the way Spieth blends his youth with a refreshing maturity, and those who know him best—his family, his high school buddies, his former teachers—bet he'll stay that way.

Spieth's number-one fan is his sister, Ellie, who is 14 and autistic. The feeling is mutual, and Spieth's concern for her borders on the legendary. His former golf coach at Jesuit High School in Dallas, Carly Marino, describes him as "one of the guys" and "a regular high school kid"—even as he was the national Junior Golfer of the Year.

Jesuit High president Michael Earsing put it this way: "I think it's a hope of everybody who works in Catholic education that you see somebody who's achieving at such a high level, who is also a wonderful model for our students."

Wisdom is with the humble. (Proverbs 11:2)

Keep me humble always, Father.

Who Will Carry Me?

Ten-year-old Ella Frech lost the use of her legs in 2014 due to a virus. Though she's adapted well to her new reality, including becoming a wheelchair athlete, there are certain things she can't do—like go into the water at the beach by herself.

One Sunday, her mother Rebecca carried her into the water, and Ella asked, "How will I get down to the water when I'm too heavy or you're too old to carry me?" Rebecca answered that her friends will carry her. Ella found this hard to believe.

As she recalled on her Patheos blog, Rebecca responded, "There will be lots of people who come and go in your life, Ella, but the ones you hang onto are the ones who would carry you...There are times when life is hard and grown-ups need help too... Our friends help us to carry our sadness or our anger or our worry. Even people who can walk need to be carried sometimes."

Those kinds of friends, Rebecca concluded, will be God's gift to Ella: "And they won't just be your legs. They will be a part of your heart."

A friend loves at all times. (Proverbs 17:17)

Inspire me to be a friend who will carry others when they're down, Lord.

Tarmac Pizza Party

You've likely heard stories about airline passengers experiencing nightmarish delays on the tarmac that left them stranded for hours with nothing to eat or drink. Thankfully, some airlines are learning that they need to treat their customers in these situations with more patience and consideration.

Consider the example of a Delta flight from Philadelphia to Atlanta in May 2015 that was diverted to Knoxville, Tennessee, due to a torrential downpour. Instead of letting passengers grow frustrated at the delay, the flight crew instead ordered pizza for everyone. Based on social media posts from people on the plane, that simple gesture picked up everyone's spirits.

On Twitter, Riley Vasquez wrote, "We are sitting on a runway stuck on a Delta flight because of weather. So they're throwing us a pizza party!" Delta spokesman Morgan Durrant explained, "It's part of an effort company-wide…to get food and beverages to delayed customers."

All people want to feel respected. Sometimes all it takes is kindness, consideration—and a helping of pizza.

Do not withhold kindness. (Sirach 7:33)

Bless the frustrated with models of kindness, Father.

Praying on the Fourth of July

Picnics and parades are great ways to celebrate the Fourth of July, but *Guideposts* magazine's Bob Hostetler offers several other suggestions for working prayer into the festivities as well:

- "When you see the 'Stars and Stripes,' don't just cheer or salute; give thanks for your freedom even as you pray for those who don't enjoy the same freedoms you do."

- "If you watch a parade, let the procession remind you...of the cost of freedom in the past and beauty of freedom in the present. Then pray for the spread of freedom in the future."

- "When you see military uniforms, give thanks for those who have sacrificed in the past and serve in the present to obtain and protect the freedoms you enjoy. But pray also for peace among nations and all people."

- "If you indulge in a holiday cookout...say a prayer of thanks to God for the hot dogs, chips, corn-on-the-cob and watermelon. But also ask Him to bless and prosper those farmers, grocers, and others who helped bring the food to your table."

Happy is the nation whose God is the Lord. (Psalm 33:12)

May we always remain "one nation under God," Creator.

Day of Deliverance

American founding father John Adams knew that he and his colleagues had accomplished something historic when they declared their independence from Great Britain on July 2, 1776, and then finally approved the Declaration of Independence on July 4th. In a letter to his wife Abigail, Adams stated:

"I am apt to believe that it will be celebrated by succeeding generations as the great anniversary festival. It ought to be commemorated, as the Day of Deliverance by solemn Acts of Devotion to God Almighty. It ought to be solemnized with pomp and parade, with shows, games, sports, guns, bells, bonfires and illuminations from one end of this continent to the other...

"You will think me transported with enthusiasm but I am not. I am well aware of the toil and blood and treasure, that it will cost us to maintain this Declaration, and support and defend these States. Yet through all the gloom I can see the rays of ravishing light and glory. I can see that the end is more than worth all the means."

For freedom Christ has set us free.
(Galatians 5:1)

May we never take for granted our hard-won freedoms, Lord, or the inherent dignity we possess as Your children.

A Talker Who Loves His Job

Father James Keller would have appreciated Marco Bedoya. Among other things, the Maryknoll priest who founded The Christophers in 1945 was famous for declaring that everyone had a job to do that was meant for no one else. He would have found a kindred soul in Bedoya, who ushers tourists to see the Statue of Liberty and who absolutely loves his job.

"I've never seen him have a bad day," says his supervisor, and he's got a favorite word for all the people he meets: friend.

Bedoya was profiled in a story by Lisa Colangelo in the *Daily News.* He's 47 years old, was born in Ecuador but raised in France, and is fluent in seven languages. As manager of guest services for Statue Cruises, which runs the tourist boats to Liberty and Ellis islands, he's got the ideal job for meeting people from all over the world and simply yakking it up.

"I love to talk," says Bedoya, who speaks English, Spanish, French, German, Japanese, Italian, and Quechua, an Indian language native to the Ecuador-Peru region. "And I love this job!"

**Render service with enthusiasm.
(Ephesians 6:7)**

Infuse me with a spirit of joy in all I do, Divine Creator.

The Mysterious Mysteries

Father William Byrne of Washington, D.C., admits that from time to time he makes up his own mysteries of the rosary. Herewith are his "Mysterious Mysteries," covering the 18 years of the hidden life of Jesus as a boy and young man:

- **Keeps holy the Sabbath.** The Holy Family would have walked to temple, worshipped, visited with friends and returned home for a meal together.

- **Hangs out with friends.** Jesus was called on in school, but everyone felt better about themselves from hanging out with the Lord. "Leaving people better from an encounter with you is the blessing to pray for during this mystery."

- **Helps the neighbors.** "Picture the old lady next door to the Holy Family. I bet she never had to drag her trash cans back each week."

- **Our Lord does the dishes.** "I can picture Jesus, Mary and Joseph outdoing one another in kindness."

- **Jesus attends a wedding in Cana.** Did He have fun? Did He dance? Did He laugh? Of course... and in so doing He "helped us realize the true blessings of our hidden life."

My soul magnifies the Lord. (Luke 1:46)

May the example of Your Holy Family guide my actions, Jesus.

Pit Bull Saves the Day

It was a hot August afternoon when eight-year-old Jesse-Cole Shaver was playing near a creek behind his Oregon City apartment with about nine other children and his pit bull, Hades.

Suddenly, one of the children stepped on a rotten log, which released a swarm of angry bees. All of the kids ran away, but Jesse-Cole, who was stung about 24 times, was in too much pain to move on his own.

Luckily, Hades instantly came to the rescue. "Hades saw me and came and she dragged me up to the grass," Jesse-Cole told Oregon's *KPTV*. "[She] let me crawl on her back and then took me to mom."

Jesse-Cole and his sister Jasmine, who is allergic to bees, stayed in the hospital overnight. Thankfully, both kids were well enough to be sent home the following morning. Their mother repeatedly gave thanks to the dog who saved her children's lives.

Heroes come in all shapes and sizes, animal or human. May we be grateful to those who put their lives at risk to save others.

Do not press me to leave you...where you go, I will go. (Ruth 1:16)

Abba, bless all pets, vigilant guardians of our children.

Art Can Bring People Together

In his World War II drama *Little Boy*, executive producer Eduardo Verastegui includes two characters who form an unlikely friendship: Father Oliver, the local priest, and Hashimoto, a Japanese man who doesn't believe in God.

This story element has modern implications. During a *Christopher Closeup* interview, Verastegui explained, "I believe that art has the power to heal and bring people together. Right now, we are living in a world that is very divided with a lot of violence, war, pain, sadness, depression, and fear.

"My hope as a filmmaker is to bring people together. That's why Hashimoto has a different belief system than Father Oliver, but nonetheless they respect each other, they love each other, they help each other. That's a profound message because there's more that unites us than what divides us. Sometimes we focus on what divides us...[but] I think we can start focusing on the things we agree on—and the rest, let's still have that dialogue with respect, charity and humility."

Love one another with mutual affection. (Romans 12:10)

May I do my part to heal this world's divisions, Lord.

A Waitress Who Cares

Kayla Lane, a waitress in Fort Worth, Texas's West Side Cafe, genuinely cares about her customers. When Shaun and Debbie Riddle came in one day without their baby daughter Glory, she asked about the child. That's when the Riddles revealed that Glory had died in her sleep a few weeks ago.

Lane could see how heartbroken they were, and she grieved for them herself. As a gesture of kindness, she wrote the following message on their bill: "Your ticket has been paid for. We are terribly sorry for your loss. God Bless—The West Side."

As reported by *The Blaze*, Lane told a "white lie" because she actually paid for their meal herself. It's something she had done in the past for firefighters and military personnel. "I feel privileged that I'm able to do it," she said.

The Riddles were so impressed by Lane that they shared their story with local media to show that good people are everywhere. Debbie Riddle said, "Loss is an unexplainable tragedy, but this is proof that one person can make a difference."

The teaching of kindness is on her tongue. (Proverbs 31:26)

Divine Healer, inspire me to offer comfort to others in any way I can.

Teaching Children about Forgiveness

"I was not a kid who knew how to forgive," admits children's book author Nicole Lataif. "Yet I never thought I had a problem with forgiveness... until I became an adult."

After reading Father Scott Hurd's book *Forgiveness: A Catholic Approach*, Lataif thought it would be a good idea to introduce the concepts she had learned to children in a way they could understand. That's when she wrote her second Christopher Award-winning book *I Forgive You*, illustrated by Katy Betz.

One important concept in *I Forgive You* is summed up in the line, "God loves you. No matter what you do, He never says, 'I'm through with you.'"

That doesn't mean misbehaving doesn't have consequences, but rather that God will forgive us anything if we ask Him. "And if we can recognize how merciful God has been to us," said Lataif during a *Christopher Closeup* interview, "then we will recognize how much He loves us— and we can therefore love others in forgiveness."

One who forgives an affront fosters friendship, but one who dwells on disputes will alienate a friend. (Proverbs 17:9)

Help me to emulate Your Divine Mercy, Holy Spirit.

Alone with God

"Language has created the word loneliness to express the pain of being alone, and solitude to express the glory of being alone." This comment by theologian Paul Tillich points out how much our feelings color our experience.

To be lonely is to feel isolated—cut off from others and locked into ourselves. It is to feel loss and sadness and self-pity.

But to experience solitude is to be alone with something, such as a book or music—or with God—in meditation or prayer. It is to feel peace and well-being.

To turn loneliness into solitude, we need to concentrate on something outside ourselves. That's why prayer can free us from isolation. It connects us with the beautiful and the universal—with God.

O my God, I cry by day, but You do not answer; and by night, but find no rest. Yet You are enthroned on the praises of Israel. In You our ancestors...trusted, and You delivered them. (Psalm 22:2-4)

Lord, transform my loneliness into comforting solitude with You.

A Helping Hand—and Much More

Sometimes a small act of kindness is far bigger than we think. For instance, truck driver Will Maguire once stopped to help a stranded motorist on a Maryland highway. He saw that the woman was very upset so he reassured her. Then he fixed her flat tire. When she offered to pay her rescuer, he graciously refused.

What Maguire didn't know was that the motorist had been raped several years before. Her memories of that horrific incident remained fresh as she sat alone in her car after her tire blew. She felt overwhelmed with fear as the traffic roared past. Then, a good-hearted stranger gave her a helping hand.

"Even if he didn't see why what he had done made him so great, to me he was a hero," the woman said later. "He stopped and cared."

Stopping and caring seems like a huge effort some days, but the good you do is not always clear. A little thing can mean the whole world to someone in need of what you can give.

Blessed are the merciful, for they will receive mercy. (Matthew 5:7)

Show us who needs our merciful help, Lord.

Sticky Question

Few people heard of George de Mestral. The Swiss-born inventor died in February, 1990, and his obituary was on the back pages of newspapers, if at all.

He received his first patent at age 12, and spent years perfecting the fastener we know as Velcro. The name is a combination of "velvet" and "crochet," the latter a French word for "hook." Velcro fasteners are made of two strips of nylon, one consisting of tiny loops, the other covered with tiny hooks.

When pressed together, the strips cling to each other, much as thistle burrs cling to clothing. In fact it was a walk in the woods in 1941 that led to the development of Velcro. De Mestral came out of the wooded area outside of Geneva with burrs sticking to his clothing and wondered why.

After seven years of research, he knew. Today Velcro is used to fasten everything from clothing to artificial hearts and the manufacturer says it will still hold fast after being fastened as much as fifty thousand times. The lesson? An inquisitive mind is behind the progress of civilization.

Search, and you will find. (Matthew 7:7)

Bless me with an inquisitive mind, Creator.

To the Parents of Young Children...

"To the Parents of Our Young Children, May We Suggest..." is a list of suggestions that churches around the country have put into their parish bulletins. It reads:

"Relax! God put the wiggle in children. Don't feel you have to suppress it in God's house. Sit toward the front where it is easier for your little ones to see and hear what's going on at the altar. They tire of seeing the backs of others' heads.

"Quietly explain the parts of the Mass and actions of the priest, altar servers, choir, etc. Sing the hymns, pray and voice the responses. Children learn liturgical behavior by copying you.

"If you have to leave Mass with your child, feel free to do so, but please come back. As Jesus said, 'Let the children come to me.'

"Remember that the way we welcome children in church directly affects the way they respond to the Church, to God, and to one another. Let them know that they are at home in this house of worship."

Out of the mouths of infants and nursing babies, You have prepared praise for yourself. (Matthew 21:16)

May our churches nurture children in their faith, Savior.

Chairman of the Barangay

Super Typhoon Haiyan brought devastation to the Philippines in November 2013, leaving many families trapped in evacuation centers without food. Ric De Veyra, who waited out the storm in a shelter with hundreds of people, said, "I saw no more houses, no more grass. I didn't know what to do."

But De Veyra had just been elected chairman of his "barangay" (community), so it was up to him to take care of his neighbors despite the fact that his wife and sons were at a different shelter. He led the efforts to clear the roads so relief food could get through.

De Veyra also appealed to Catholic Relief Services for help in building new homes, insisting that his neighbors get houses before him. He told CRS's Jen Hardy, "It didn't matter if people voted for me or not. We all needed safe and dry places to sleep."

De Veyra, his wife, and their four sons finally moved into their new home in July 2014. His community is grateful for his leadership under pressure.

Whoever wishes to become great among you must be your servant. (Mark 10:43)

Keep me calm and focused during life's storms, Father.

The Man in the Dumpster

Patheos blogger Tom Zampino's family knew it was time to get rid of a lot of the "stuff" they had accumulated in their home: toys, books, clothes, etc. They rented a dumpster, put it in their driveway, and began the rigorous throwing-away process.

One day, Zampino was surprised to find a man he recognized from the neighborhood inside the dumpster. This man spoke no English and looked fearful, as if he was expecting to get yelled at. Then, Zampino noticed the items the man had set aside: "Toys still fit for some little girl," he wrote. "And clothes perhaps for that same child."

Zampino just smiled at him and told him, "Be careful." The appreciative man smiled back and continued rummaging. He returned on other days, and the family always left him alone.

One morning, Zampino came outside to cut up a dirty old carpet that he had left next to the dumpster because it was too heavy to lift in one piece. Yet, the entire carpet now lay in the dumpster. Zampino realized his new friend had done him an unrequested favor, a favor that reaffirmed his belief that kindness is a two-way street.

Show kindness...to one another. (Zechariah 7:9)

Holy Spirit, renew the face of the earth with kindness.

Honeymooners Need Help

Honeymoons are supposed to be happy, carefree experiences, but that wasn't the case for newlyweds Valasia Limnioti and Konstantinos Patronis. The Greek couple's trip to New York City during Greece's July 2015 debt crisis left them penniless because their credit cards kept being declined.

Thankfully, they had prepaid for their flight and hotel, but they could no longer cover ordinary expenses. As reported by *NBC News*, the couple decided to reach out to the Greek Orthodox Archdiocese of America, which contacted several churches in Astoria, New York. St. Demetrios Greek Orthodox church and St. Irene Chrysovalantou supplied the travelers with several hundred dollars.

The grateful but proud couple expressed embarrassment at needing the money, but Rev. Vasilios Louros of St. Demetrios told them, "Don't worry, that's why we're here. This is the church of Christ and we always help people."

They are to do good, to be rich in good works, generous, and ready to share. (1 Timothy 6:18)

Remind me, Lord, that when I serve others, I serve You.

God's Healing Ways

On September 11, 2011, 14-year-old Taylor Hale of Waukee, Iowa, was goofing around with a friend when she fell off the hood of his car while he was trying to drive away. Six days later, she suffered a brain hemorrhage. Doctors fought to save her life, until part of her brain sank into her spinal cord, at which point she was declared brain dead.

As the family assembled to say goodbye, Jeff Stickel, a friend of Taylor's parents and a chiropractor who felt God was calling him to treat Taylor, came to visit them at the hospital. Taylor's parents were against Stickel intervening, so he simply placed his hands on Taylor's neck and asked God to heal her.

Later that day, Taylor was taken off life support. She astonished everyone when she gasped for breath! Life support was reconnected, brain activity increased, and she fluttered her eyes and mumbled. Four years later, Taylor graduated from high school. "God can save people," she told *USA Today*. "I'm thankful to all the doctors and nurses and therapists who helped me get better. But God did most of the saving."

You have healed me. (Psalm 30:2)

Lord, help us to have faith in Your healing ways.

Keeping Faith Alive at College

How do you keep your kids close to the Church once they go off to college? That's a real concern for many parents. Studies show that close to a third of those who reach maturity give up the ghost along the way—and collegians are particularly vulnerable.

When Anthony Gockowski wrote "10 tips for college-bound Catholics," the first thing he mentioned was "pray daily." It's important to set a schedule for daily prayer, formal or informal. It'll keep students on the straight and narrow.

Other hints Gockowski offers: seek accountability, step outside of yourself, serve others, get into an exercise habit.

It's important to read good books, too, to learn more about yourself and your religious habits. Stand firm as well, for college has a way of testing your faith. And make your education your own by studying what you want. Get in the habit of Sunday Mass and confession.

Good companions are all-important. Most campuses have a Newman Center or some other good place to start. And that gets us back to where it all began: pray every day. Good luck!

Devote yourselves to prayer. (Colossians 4:2)

Jesus, remind me to nurture my relationship with You.

A Hometown Hero

When James Thompson, a conductor for the railroad in the New York City borough of Staten Island, first saw the girl, she was on a platform not far from where he was standing. She was a teenager—distraught and talking on a cell phone about the darkest of plans.

"She was obviously very upset," he told Pete Donohue of the *Daily News.* "I overheard her several times saying she was going to kill herself."

As he hurried to her side, he called the rail control center, alerting railway motormen and summoning the police. Then he asked the girl to tell him about her troubles. She did—and he mostly listened, for what seemed an eternity, until the cops arrived.

"I have a 19-year-old daughter," he said later. "If she was ever in that situation, I hope there would be somebody there to help."

Thompson himself was a help that day, and might have saved a life in the process. For his actions, he was nominated for a "Hometown Heroes" award.

When the righteous cry for help, the Lord hears, and rescues them from all their troubles. (Psalm 34:17)

Save us from the depths of despair, Light of Life.

Like Jesus in a War Zone

"He's Jesus Christ." That's the unexpected way a Muslim paramount chief in the Nuba Mountains of Sudan described Catholic doctor Tom Catena. His reasoning is that Jesus healed the sick, which is what "Dr. Tom" does every day.

Nicholas Kristof in *The New York Times* notes the overwhelming challenges under which Dr. Tom, who hails from Amsterdam, New York, works. "He is the only doctor permanently based in the Nuba Mountains for a population of more than half a million people."

There is no electricity or running water. And Sudan's government regularly bombs the area to crush a rebellion there, leaving Dr. Tom to "pry out shrapnel from women's flesh and amputate limbs of children, even as he also delivers babies and removes appendixes."

For his hard work, Dr. Tom earns just $350 a month. So why does he do it? He said, "I've been given benefits from the day I was born. A loving family. A great education. So I see it as an obligation, as a Christian and as a human being, to help."

Is there no balm in Gilead? Is there no physician there? (Jeremiah 8:22)

Bless doctors who care for the desperate and needy, Lord.

Can a Sinner Be a Saint?

Vincent McKenna smokes, drinks, gambles, curses, and cavorts with a prostitute. Yet his 12-year-old neighbor Oliver thinks he's a modern-day saint. And he might be right.

That's the story behind *St. Vincent*, a 2014 comedy starring Bill Murray that earned a Christopher Award for its recognition that being a saint doesn't mean you were never a sinner.

As their friendship develops, Oliver sees a good-heartedness in Vincent that he rarely shows the world, especially in the way he secretly cares for his wife who is in a medical facility due to Alzheimer's. And Vincent comes to care about Oliver, while teaching him to defend himself from bullies.

When Oliver is given an assignment in his Catholic school to write about someone he considers a modern-day saint, he chooses Vincent. Though it seems a stretch, his tribute becomes the emotional heart of the movie that will leave you nodding your head in agreement and maybe even tearing up a little.

St. Vincent is an edgy and endearing film that shows viewers how the love of a makeshift family can help anyone's halo shine a little brighter.

You are citizens with the saints. (Ephesians 2:9)

You call each of us to sainthood, Lord. Guide my path.

Keep Your Strengths — Strong

It's natural for people to emphasize their strong points. But, strengths taken to extremes can turn into problems.

Hollywood produce Dore Schary had this to say: "A person who calls himself frank and candid can very easily find himself becoming tactless and cruel. A person who prides himself on being tactful can find eventually that he has become evasive and deceitful.

"A person with firm convictions can become pig-headed. A person who is inclined to be temperate and judicious can sometimes turn into someone with weak convictions...Loyalty can lead to fanaticism. Caution can become timidity. Freedom can become license. Confidence can become arrogance. Humility can become servility. All these are ways in which strength can become weakness."

That's a good reminder to take stock of your strong points and your weak ones—and never let the latter overshadow the former.

My grace is sufficient for you, for power is made perfect in weakness. (2 Corinthians 12:9)

Divine Savior, help us transform even the worst of our weaknesses into holy strengths.

Recovering After Tragedy

When Victoria Commock of Coral Gables, Florida, heard about the bombing of the Federal Building in Oklahoma City in 1995, her first reaction was: Go there.

Having survived her own tragedy—her husband, John, died aboard Pan Am Flight 103 when the plane exploded over Lockerbie, Scotland—Commock was convinced of the need to help others get through similar circumstances.

"Really, what I do is to talk with people," she said. "I listen to the widows and widowers, to the parents who are having nightmares about raising children by themselves. And I can say to them, 'Yeah, that happened to me.'"

Commock knows firsthand how such caring conversations can help. Shortly after Lockerbie, a woman in London called to see how she was doing. That woman had lost her own husband in the bombing of a London department store. She told Commock that it would get better. It did. "It is so important to see that other people who have been where you are have managed to live a full life again," she said.

Support the weak. (Acts 20:35)

Lord, help us to rise above our tragedies, stronger than ever.

Saying 'Yes' to the Other Bride's Dress

Elizabeth Jensen, the seventh of eight children and a full-time student at Brigham Young University, was set to be married in the spring of 2015. But she couldn't afford a wedding dress, at least not the one of her dreams, which had a price tag of $480. "My dad has been unemployed for a while," she told the *Deseret News*. "The cost of things adds up."

While she was in the store, another bride-to-be approached the storeowner and asked if any of the other brides needed some help. As *Yahoo! News* reported, the stranger didn't find her own dress that day, but decided to purchase Jensen's for her.

She kept herself anonymous, which is why Jensen came forward with the story, because she wanted the woman to know, as she said, "how grateful I am and how special she will be to me."

When Jensen learned the dress was being purchased for her, she burst into tears. "The fact there was someone in the store watching me and seeing how much I loved the dress and taking the time," she said. "It's something I'll never forget."

Whoever is kind to the poor lends to the Lord, and will be repaid in full. (Proverbs 19:17)

Divine Giver, instill us with generous hearts.

Academics, Athletics, Spiritual Formation

When Walter Kirimitsu took over as head of St. Louis school in Honolulu, Hawaii, he vowed to do something about its reputation as a "football school." Last year, as he prepared at age 74 to retire as head administrator, he had surpassed his goal.

Kirimitsu restored a Hawaiian cultural program, and saw a dramatic increase in art, drama and music classes. Finally—in what he referred to as the "hallmark" of the school's academic improvement—he oversaw construction of the $12 million Clarence T.C. Ching Learning and Technology Center. The three-story building is the first new classroom structure at the school in more than 80 years.

Kirimitsu saw to it that other endeavors weren't overlooked, either. "They are all equally important," he told the *Hawaii Catholic Herald*, "academics, athletics and spiritual formation. We made sure that the Catholic Marianist mission is integrated into our curriculum." An attorney and former judge, he intends to devote his time in retirement to community service, focusing in those areas. That, he said, and golf.

Commit your work to the Lord. (Proverbs 16:3)

Let my dreams and goals build hope for future generations, Divine Teacher.

A Most Precious Gift

When two-year-old Greta Greene was unexpectedly killed by bricks falling from a New York building, her heartbroken parents made yet another sacrifice. According to a story in the *Daily News*, they "made the painful decision to donate their daughter's organs as a last gift to humanity from their beautiful little girl."

More people are alive today because of what modern medicine can do with donated organs or portions of organs. There are possibilities to be a deceased donor or sometimes even a living donor (often people donate one of their kidneys).

And it's not necessary to wait for a tragedy. Organs are in short supply. You can make your wishes known today. Some people indicate their desires on their driver's license.

Start by educating yourself about what the process entails. Then make a decision based on what's right for you. You might have an opportunity to give someone else a precious gift.

A new heart I will give you, and a new spirit I will put within you. (Ezekiel 36:26)

Guide us in making the right decisions regarding modern medical choices, Divine Creator.

Dolphin Tale Brings Healing

Injury and illness can leave you feeling like there's no way to move forward with life, but one dolphin proved otherwise.

The 2011 movie *Dolphin Tale* was inspired by the true story of Winter, a female dolphin whose tail needed to be amputated after it was damaged in a crab trap. The head biologist at Florida's Clearwater Marine Aquarium, which rescued the dolphin, realized Winter would need a prosthetic to swim, but it took months of trial and error to create a version she would use.

As reported by *Catholic Digest's* Daria Sockey, sharing that story with the world brought many visitors to Clearwater to see Winter, and also created a number of little "miracles."

She wrote, "Children who themselves were amputees found the courage to go through the painful process of learning to use a prosthetic leg or arm." Wounded warriors from Iraq and Afghanistan also came to embrace a new beginning for their lives. *Dolphin Tale* director David Yates calls these responses "a gift from God," one that will continue to keep on giving.

**See, everything has become new!
(2 Corinthians 5:17)**

Give those who are injured the courage to move forward with their lives, Jesus.

A Tenor's Guide to Life

It's been a tough climb to the top for tenor Bryan Hymel, but he looks back on the struggle with a sense of appreciation and a touch of humor. "I thought," said Hymel, "that within five years I'd be one of the 'Three Tenors.' And that's not the way it goes. It's been quite a journey."

Years ago Hymel, a native of New Orleans, decided to give it "one more shot" after a long period of taking any kind of singing job just to pay the rent. That shot paid off. Now Hymel, 35, can take satisfaction in a career in which he's performed operas worldwide, sung at the Met, and has contracts to sing well into 2020.

He sees the hand of God in it all, he told Christine Bordelon of the New Orleans *Clarion Herald*. "Art is there to hold a mirror up to life," he said, considering what he does as a tenor is using his God-given talents to tell stories of redemption, love and self-sacrifice. "The gifts one has," he said, "are a reflection of the gifts given."

**Rekindle the gift of God that is within you.
(2 Timothy 1:6)**

Sustain me in my struggles, Lord, and lead me to success.

A Traffic Stop to Remember

One July morning, Police Chief Whitney Whitworth of Thrall, Texas, turned on his flashing red lights while patrolling a local street to let the car in front of him know it should pull over. But this was no ordinary vehicle he was stopping; it was a Ford F150 Hot Wheels Truck driven by 12-year-old Sierra Koehne and her brother Bryce.

Chief Whitworth strolled over to Sierra and asked for her license. She just smiled and said she didn't have one. Instead of booking her, the officer gave her a Beanie Baby and sent her on her way. Sierra was left charmed and amused.

As reported by *KTBC TV*, Chief Whitworth admits he's a bit of a prankster, but he thinks that small acts of kindness with neighborhood kids— and the community in general—are ways to build a better relationship between police and the public. Sierra's mother Erin agrees, saying, "They make themselves well-known just by…stopping to tell you hi, they're very friendly."

To build better relationships in your community, be friendly and say hi. It's a simple but meaningful gesture.

Come over, friend; sit down here. (Ruth 4:1)

May I always be open to making new friends, Jesus.

The Trip That Led to a Calling

Katy Betz grew up admiring the illustrations she saw in popular books like *The Berenstain Bears* series, but it wasn't until a trip to Europe as an 18-year-old college student that she realized she wanted to make art her career.

During an interview on *Christopher Closeup*, she recalled, "Going to Italy, seeing the Vatican and the Sistine Chapel—and even in France, the Gothic cathedrals and the stories of the Bible in the stained glass windows—that to me was saying, 'This is a way to communicate God's truth and His redemption.' I realized, 'This is my calling. I need to do this.'"

That passion and talent, especially for creating illustrations that connect with children, led Betz and author Nicole Lataif to a Christopher Award win for their book *I Forgive You*, for kids ages four to eight.

Betz cherished the opportunity to be part of a project that reflects her faith: "Some of my freelance work is commercial and there's no underlying moral, necessarily. With *I Forgive You*, I felt like I was able to glorify God through [my work]."

Consider your own call. (1 Corinthians 1:26)

Open my eyes to see the road that You're calling me to follow, Lord.

Tankchair

"Go on without me." Those four words from his wheelchair-bound wife Liz inspired combat veteran Brad Soden to do the impossible.

A 1999 car accident left Liz paralyzed from the waist down. During a trip to Arizona's Hualapai Mountain Park in 2001, the couple and their five kids wanted to go camping but couldn't push the wheelchair through the dirt and mud. Liz told her family to go on without her, but Brad refused. Instead, he grew determined to solve the problem.

Despite having no formal engineering training, Brad spent years developing what is now called the Tankchair. It's a wheelchair that uses wide treads like a tank. Though it costs $15,000 to produce, it's bringing joy and mobility to Liz and many others, including injured servicemen and women. Profits go back into the company for more research and development.

Brad told *Bloomberg News,* "I get more pleasure watching other people have fun. You see a kid smile, or you see happiness, and the tears of it...It's just really cool."

Nothing will be impossible with God.
(Luke 1:37)

When a goal seems impossible, show me the way, Lord.

A Mission from God

Over 2,000 migrants drowned in the Mediterranean in 2014 while riding in unsafe boats meant to help them escape war-torn Libya for a better life in Europe. In response, a couple in Malta, Regina Catrambone and her husband Chris, created the Migrant Offshore Aid Station (MOAS) to prevent future disasters.

As reported by England's *Catholic Herald*, the privately funded group was partially inspired when the Catambrones were sailing in the Mediterranean and saw a winter jacket floating in the water. They realized it belonged to somebody who had likely drowned. Then, after hearing Pope Francis on TV asking entrepreneurs to help those in need, the couple chose to take the initiative and start MOAS, naming their ship The Phoenix.

The *Herald* reported, "The couple inaugurated the mission by opening the ship with a Mass…The priest then told the assembled crew that they were on a mission from God. When the ship comes across a migrant boat, the crew will contact the nearest authorities. They will then approach the boats and hand out food, water, lifejackets and medical assistance."

Do not withhold good from those to whom it is due, when it is in your power to do it. (Proverbs 3:27)

Guide refugees to peace and safety, Lord.

Making Sense of Cents

For many of us, money and fear go hand-in-hand: Do I have enough? Will I run out? If I had a little more money, my worries would be over.

Writer Barbara Bartocci gathered a group of friends, all at various places in the "money market." They agreed to meet weekly for six months to discuss attitudes about money. They made the following discoveries:

- Most people have no idea why they spend the way they do. Many times we are motivated by unexamined emotions: stress, or the need for attention.
- Wants are not the same as needs.
- Who you are does not depend on what you own.
- Become part of the cycle of giving and receiving and your needs will be met.

> **Give me neither poverty nor riches; feed me with the food that I need, or I shall be full, and deny You, and say, "Who is the Lord?"**
> **(Proverbs 30:8-9)**

May we never give any earthly idol precedence over You, Jesus.

Honoring Our Elders

We stand to learn much from Native Americans, especially with regard to the elderly. At the San Xavier del Blanc mission near Tucson, Arizona, Betty Calvert observed how her 94-year-old mother, frail and small, moved among other worshipers, most of whom were Indians.

Calvert watched as her mother approached, and the Indians dropped to their knees to ask for her blessing. Some whispered, "Vaya con Dios" (Go with God) as she made the sign of the cross over them, while her daughter looked on in amazement.

Later at home, Calvert's mother told her, "The Indians...revere their elders. They believe all the wisdom and knowledge an old person has acquired can be passed on through a blessing or a loving touch."

What a lovely belief. It's not too late to learn from our elders and ask for their blessing.

Rise before the aged, and defer to the old. (Leviticus 19:32)

Jesus, help us to learn from those who have come before us.

The Sweet, Fundamental Things

Laura Ingalls Wilder is best known as the author of the *Little House on the Prairie* book series, which became the basis of the much-loved television show starring Michael Landon and Melissa Gilbert. But Wilder had been writing for 20 years before she ever started that work.

When Stephen Hines of Nashville, Tennessee, discovered that fact, he made a trip to Missouri in search of those early writings. He was on a personal journey as well. Having recently lost his job, Hines felt abandoned by God and worried about providing for his family.

Hines found answers in Wilder's wisdom. "It is the simple things of life," she wrote, "that make living worthwhile, the sweet fundamental things such as love and duty, work and rest."

"As I read those words," Hines said, "I could almost feel the presence of this deeply Christian woman. My worries and hurt over losing my job seemed inconsequential now. God was with me, and together we would bring to others this message that so many seemed to have forgotten."

In quietness and trust shall be your strength. (Isaiah 30:15)

Messiah, may I always treasure the simple things in life.

When Calls the Heart

Brian Bird has been a writer and producer in Hollywood for 30 years, working on shows like *Touched by an Angel*. His latest project is the Hallmark Channel series *When Calls the Heart*, which is based on the novel by Janette Oke. The show takes place in 1910 and tells the story of Elizabeth Thatcher, a young teacher accustomed to high society life, who gets assigned to a frontier town called Coal Valley. She makes new friends there, but also faces surprising challenges.

During a *Christopher Closeup* interview, Bird described his approach to storytelling: "All human beings have violin strings running through our souls. These strings, when you pluck them, they reverberate with certain themes like forgiveness, sacrifice, courage, and banding together to help one another."

Bird also believes the series provides an opportunity to bring families together: "We're all off in our little rooms watching TV by ourselves now. That's not a good thing. We need to balance that with some shared family experiences. I hope that our show is [something] families can take advantage of."

My heart overflows with a goodly theme. (Psalm 45:1)

Bless storytellers with talent and wisdom, Lord.

Service Makes You Smile

Though Danielle Rizzo was diagnosed with autism at age four, she's able to perform acts of kindness just like anyone else. Her parents, David and Mercedes, made sure to be models of giving themselves, and have guided Danielle toward taking part in charity projects. For instance, she donated her hair to Locks of Love, which makes wigs for children with cancer.

Mercedes also helped Danielle perform an act of service in their local New Jersey supermarket. A woman in a motorized shopping cart asked Mercedes if Danielle could help her unload her cart onto the cashier's counter. Realizing that this was a perfect opportunity for Danielle to give of herself, Mercedes responded, "She will help you, and I will help you, too."

During a *Christopher Closeup* interview, Mercedes said, "I had to prompt [Danielle]—'Put the bread up on the counter'—but when it was over, I was filled with wonder and awe because she was able to do that. And Danielle was smiling and so happy to be of service! I think we forget sometimes that folks with special needs love to be of service to others."

We have gifts that differ according to the grace given to us. (Romans 12:6)

Increase my joy in being of service to others, Lord.

Thanks for the Hard Time

At the 1996 Summer Olympics in Atlanta, the world cheered for its greatest athletes, many of whom had overcome personal obstacles to get there. Swimmers from the USA were not favored to win. But they beat the odds and won more swimming medals than any other country.

One of these underdogs was Amy Van Dyken. An asthmatic, she never swims with more than two-thirds of her lung capacity. As a teen, she couldn't walk up a flight of stairs without getting winded. Her high school teammates refused to swim relays with her because she was too slow.

After she won four gold medals, Van Dyken said cheerfully, "Those girls who gave me such a hard time, I want to thank you. Here I am! This is a victory for all the nerds out there."

Amy Van Dyken is a fine example of someone who didn't let negative attitudes affect her. She believed in herself enough to accomplish her dreams.

Don't let others stop you—go for the gold!

Do not fear. Only believe. (Luke 8:50)

Provide us with courage to realize our dreams, Father.

The Footprints You're Leaving

Since winning *American Idol* in 2002, Kelly Clarkson has built an amazing career for herself in the music industry. Unlike many pop stars, she found success without going down the road of sexually explicit lyrics and imagery.

In 2015, Clarkson recorded the song *I Had a Dream*, which includes lyrics that challenge artists who overindulge in sexual imagery. The lyrics include the following lines: "Remember that the footprints you're leaving / Will tell us all who you really are. / It's too bad you can't see what you're worth…Character is shown by the things that we do. / The one thing you're never gonna hide is the truth."

Good for Clarkson for aiming high and trying to accomplish something positive through her music. Artists don't always hit the mark they're aiming for, but noble attempts may eventually lead to something good, leaving young women with the message that they don't need to exploit their bodies in order to be successful.

Let your adornment be the inner self.
(1 Peter 3:4)

Guide the creators of modern culture, Holy Spirit, to instill a respect for people's bodies and souls.

Mission at Nuremberg

If there is a group of people in modern history who are thought of as irredeemable, it's the Nazis. Yet at the end of World War II, two American Army chaplains — Rev. Henry Gerecke, a Lutheran minister, and Father Sixtus O'Connor, a Catholic priest — made an unprecedented attempt to save the souls of the Nazi leaders held at Nuremberg prison.

Their little-known story has now been documented by Tim Townsend in the book *Mission at Nuremberg*. He writes that Rev. Gerecke wouldn't accept fake attempts at penitence:

"These were men who had spit on the notion of traditional Christianity while promoting an idea that a cleansed Germany would mean a better world and a more pure future. They had broken a contract with God, set down in the Ten Commandments, and Gerecke believed his duty as a Christian minister was to bring redemption to these souls, to save as many Nazis as he could before their executions."

More of the story tomorrow.

The wages of sin is death. (Romans 6:23)

There are crimes that seem unforgivable, Lord. Bring their perpetrators to true repentance and redemption.

A Nazi Kneels

One of the Nazis to whom Rev. Gerecke ministered was Wilhelm Keitel. As a young man, Keitel had lived an average life. He wanted to become a farmer until his father "pushed him into the army." Eventually, he became Hitler's general field marshal, whom *Mission at Nuremberg* author Tim Townsend describes as "the archetypal Nazi bootlicker."

Though Keitel had fallen in love with adulation and power, prison humbled him. A sliver of his humanity remained when he met Rev. Gerecke, who was able to convince him to rethink the crimes he had committed as a Nazi officer.

Townsend said, "Keitel asked Gerecke if he could celebrate Communion under the Chaplain's direction...He kneeled by the cot in his cell and confessed his sins. 'On his knees and under deep emotional stress, [Keitel] received the Body and Blood of our Savior,' Gerecke wrote later. 'With tears in his voice he said, 'You have helped me more than you know. May Christ, my Savior, stand by me all the way. I shall need Him so much.'"

More of the story tomorrow.

I am sorry for my sin. (Psalm 38:18)

Humble the proud and lead them home to You, Lord.

Caring for Souls on the Battlefield

While Rev. Gerecke ministered to Nazis with a Protestant background, Franciscan priest Father Sixtus O'Connor handled the Catholics. During a *Christopher Closeup* interview, *Mission at Nuremberg* author Tim Townsend said:

"[Father O'Connor] was a younger guy [who] was part of a fighting unit that marched all the way through Europe. He got a Silver Star for bravery for counseling men on the battlefield for what was then called battle fatigue, but what we would now call post-traumatic stress disorder. As bullets were flying all around him, he was trying to help people through it.

"At the end of the war, his unit helped liberate Mauthausen concentration camp in Austria, so he buried thousands and thousands of concentration camp victims. Two months later in Nuremberg, he was counseling Ernst Kaltenbrunner, who was in charge of the entire concentration camp system."

So why did Father O'Connor and Rev. Gerecke choose to help those whose actions they found repulsive? The conclusion of their story tomorrow.

When you have sinned, repent. (Sirach 18:21)

Help me put the needs of others ahead of my own, Lord.

A Spiritual Responsibility

Part of the reason that Rev. Gerecke and Father O'Connor ministered to the Nazis at Nuremberg was because they were trying to show that the United States was more civilized than its enemies. For the two men personally, however, it required an enormous amount of compassion and mercy to see the Nazis as human beings instead of monsters.

Mission at Nuremberg author Tim Townsend believes it was their deep devotion to their faith that allowed them to do so. He said, "I could not have even walked into one of those cells, I don't think. They not only walked in, but knelt on the concrete floor next to these men and prayed with them and tried to bring them back to some sort of belief in the church and in Jesus.

"That's an amazing thing to contemplate and I think it is a testament to their faith as Christians, but also to their abilities as pastors. They knew they had a particular responsibility and a calling that they took very seriously, and this was an extraordinary moment in history...They were willing to share their faith with the worst people in the world."

Overcome evil with good. (Romans 12:21)

Lead us out of darkness into Your glorious light, Savior.

Changing the Face of Beauty

As photographer Katie Driscoll looked through back-to-school ads, she noticed that none of the children resembled her daughter Grace, who has Down Syndrome. Why weren't kids with disabilities represented in these photos, she wondered?

Instead of waiting for an answer, Driscoll created a solution. The Palos Park, Illinois mom put together her own photo shoot featuring children with a variety of physical and intellectual challenges. She told *ABC News*, "These kids are going back to school, too. Wouldn't it be great if they saw somebody who used crutches or who has Down Syndrome and they'd be able to relate to another child who might be in their classroom?"

Driscoll also co-founded the campaign "Changing the Face of Beauty," which encourages "the integration of individuals with disabilities into general advertising and the media." She concludes, "Companies don't print ads without including minorities. Children with disabilities [are] one of the largest minorities so why don't we include them when casting for ads?"

Invite the poor, the crippled, the lame, and the blind. And you will be blessed. (Luke 14:13-14)

Teach me to see the beauty in all people, Creator.

Life is a Beautiful Mess

On his fourth album, entitled *Rise*, Catholic singer-songwriter PJ Anderson wrote a song called *Beautiful Mess*, which was partially inspired by the painting of Michelangelo's *Creation of Adam*, which he keeps in his music room.

During a *Christopher Closeup* interview, he explained, "In that painting, we're all so focused on God giving life with His right hand to Adam, but we forget to look at what God is doing with His left hand. If you look, He's reaching around a woman and He's touching a baby. That woman represents Mary, and through Mary we are promised the savior, Jesus.

"In that moment that God is creating us, He knows we're going to turn from Him, that we're going to make a mess of the world. But He still loves us so much that He gives us life with His right hand and promises eternal life with His left. So although we make this mess, we are beautiful because God created us—and He can get us through that mess. There's no mess we can make that's too great for His grace to save us."

By grace you have been saved through faith. (Ephesians 2:8)

When I make a mess of my life, Lord, send me Your grace.

Padres Show Heart

The San Diego Padres drafted Matt LaChappa right after his high school graduation in 1993 because they knew the great potential he possessed as a hard-throwing left-handed pitcher. He was well on his way to fulfilling that potential when two major heart attacks on the same day derailed his life in 1996.

As reported by *NBC News*, a virus caused his heart condition, which wasn't detectable in a standard physical. LaChappa suffered permanent mobility damage and lost the ability to speak. His baseball career was over.

Priscilla Oppenheimer, director of Minor League Operations for the Padres, had grown to care about LaChappa during his time with the organization, and wanted to help his family through this ordeal. As a result, the Padres re-signed him to his original contract that year—and every year since.

The salary isn't much, but the insurance coverage is crucial because he needs 24-hour care. LaChappa occasionally attends Padres games, and still displays "his trademark smile." No doubt, he feels grateful to a team that will always be a winner in his eyes.

**He will not fail you or forsake you.
(Deuteronomy 31:6)**

Help me support others through hardship, Lord.

An Atheist's Road to God

Author and radio host Jennifer Fulwiler grew up an atheist, largely because her father was an atheist. Ironically, she credits him with giving her the foundation for her eventual conversion to Catholicism.

During an interview on *Christopher Closeup* about her book *Something Other Than God*, Fulwiler said, "He's a really wonderful, humble man, and I often say that he was one of my biggest influences in converting to Catholicism, because of his humility and selfless love. And then also, what he always taught me was to seek truth above all. Even if it's inconvenient, even if you don't like the conclusions you come to, you have to always be focused on what is true."

Finding the truth in Christianity in general—and Catholicism in particular—took a lot of effort for Fulwiler, but she is now happy that her pursuit of truth led her to her spiritual home.

Those who act in accordance with truth will prosper in all their activities. (Tobit 4:6)

Divine Wisdom, You can use both believers and nonbelievers to lead us to truth. Show us all the way.

When It Feels Good to Be Wrong

"You were wrong." In many cases, those words would be cause for embarrassment, but not for Dr. Vicente Gracias, chief of Trauma and Surgical Critical Care at New Jersey's Robert Wood Johnson University Hospital. They were words he longed to hear Timmy McDonnell say to him—and he got his wish.

In October 2014, McDonnell, a Rutgers University junior, was walking along the street when he was hit by a drunk driver and sustained a "life-threatening head injury," reported the website MyCentralJersey.com. Dr. Rachana Tyagi, the neurosurgeon who performed emergency surgery on him, noted that he almost died many times. Dr. Gracias delivered a dire prognosis to the family, but hoped he would be proven wrong.

The medical staff managed to keep McDonnell alive, while his family and friends supplied the faith and hope. His mother Clare said, "All denominations and faiths under the sun stopped by to pray for Timmy. Our faith in God is what got us through."

McDonnell's recovery continues, but doctors say he's a "miracle."

Turn, O Lord, save my life. (Psalm 6:4)

Hear my prayers for health, Divine Healer.

Runner Loses Race, Wins at Life

Seth Goldstein was feeling pretty good. The 17-year-old cross country runner from Memphis's Cooper Yeshiva School was in the middle of a heated race with a chance at winning. All of a sudden, he saw a runner from the competing school fall down and start writhing on the floor. Everyone else kept running, but Goldstein immediately knelt down beside the boy to help.

"I was in shock," Jessica Chandler, a parent from the rival school, declared to Tennessee's *Knox News*. "But this guy [Seth] was taking complete control. He was like, 'You—call 911. You—go get some ice...' I thought he was a parent or EMT."

Not even the paramedics knew that Goldstein was a participant in the race until he asked them if he could finish it after they arrived. And finish it he did, with everyone from both schools cheering him on from the sidelines.

"It's an example of the values we're trying to instill in our kids," Gil Perl, dean of Cooper Yeshiva, says of his student's action. "We have the concept, from the Talmud...if you want God to have mercy on you, you have to have mercy on others."

I have finished the race. (2 Timothy 4:7)

Father, may we prize human life above all else.

Facing the Fire

Off-duty or not, one New York firefighter proved once again that he knows how to answer the bell.

Capt. William Grant was asleep in his Staten Island home when he was awakened by an explosion next door, in his neighbor's hot tub. Aided by his son, a New York police officer, he raced to help.

"We kicked the front door in, but there was so much fire and smoke and flames that we weren't able to get in," he told Michael Gartland of the *New York Post*. Instead, they ran to the back of the house, grabbed a ladder and the elder Grant climbed inside to find a woman who needed help badly.

"We had to move as fast as we could, or she probably wouldn't have survived," he said. As Grant carried his neighbor down, the ladder broke—but she survived. In a June ceremony last year, Grant was honored for his heroism.

Be strong and courageous; do not be frightened or dismayed, for the Lord your God is with you wherever you go. (Joshua 1:9)

Fill my heart with courage and my mind with wisdom, Divine Savior.

Smiles for Selfies (and Life)

These days many people enjoy taking selfies on smartphones and sharing these flattering pictures on social media. But if it weren't for specialized dentists such as Andrea Smith, there would be more people too embarrassed to be viewed in their local community, to say nothing of being broadcast worldwide.

Dr. Smith is a maxillofacial prosthodontist in Lancaster, Pennsylvania, who began doing facial restorations for cancer patients. She also helps children born with cleft lip and palate, a birth defect that affects one in every 575 children, according to an article in *Columbia* magazine by Kelly McMasters.

Dr. Smith combines her interests in art and engineering to solve potentially devastating and socially limiting health problems. "I find it very satisfying to make something (e.g. teeth) fit, to be able to find a unique solution to a problem," she said. As a highly trained professional, "I wanted to be able to say: when all hope is lost, come to me. I'll find a way to fix you."

The Lord sustains them on their sickbed; in their illness You heal all their infirmities. (Psalm 41:3)

Holy Spirit, inspire us to use our special talents to bring smiles to the faces of children.

A Lifesaving Day at the Beach

Amy Zellmer was enjoying a summer day at Lake Elmo beach in Minnesota, when she noticed a high school age lifeguard grab her rescue device and rush into the water. A two-year-old boy was by himself and looked like he was in trouble.

The lifeguard got a flotation device around the boy, swam him back to shore, and carried his limp body to the beach where she immediately started performing chest compressions. Zellmer then called 911, while her friends, who are certified in CPR and First Aid, went to help. Within two minutes, the boy was sitting up and alert with his mother at his side.

Zellmer wrote an open letter to this lifeguard on the *Huffington Post* website. She said, "You appeared shaken as you walked away, as anyone would be...Had you been a few seconds later, this story could have ended quite differently. You were alert and aware of what was going on in the water, responsible for watching what I'm guessing was a couple hundred kids at the time. I'm not sure if this is your first rescue or not—it doesn't matter. What you did was heroic, and I applaud you."

Be strong and courageous. (Joshua 1:9)

Bless lifeguards and other rescuers with good instincts and knowledge, Lord.

A Driving Force for Change

Sister Mary Louise Lynch, a Medical Mission sister who passed away in Philadelphia last year at age 89, worked a long career in social ministries.

"She was a happy blend of being compassionate and a good listener while also being a driving force for change," said a friend, Benedictine Sister Joan Marie Stief. "She was always engaged in conversation about something that would help the life of someone else, especially the poor."

Former co-chairwoman of the Baltimore Archdiocesan Justice and Peace Commission and one-time communications director for the Leadership Conference of Women Religious, she was also a chaplain for women in the Baltimore City Penitentiary and had served as a missionary in India.

Sister Lynch had a skill for making sure the people in the pews knew the importance of social justice, according to a one-time co-worker. Dick Ulrich told George Matysek of Baltimore's *Catholic Review*, "She knew the facts of what was happening around the world."

**Happy are those who observe justice.
(Psalm 106:3)**

Holy Spirit, fill me with a sense of social justice.

Doctor Brings Dose of Compassion

In the same crime-ridden part of Chicago where he grew up, Dr. Fred Richardson has run a medical clinic for 25 years. He says he's not afraid because people in the neighborhood appreciate the value of his work and keep him safe.

Dr. Richardson even makes house calls to elderly patients who can no longer get to his clinic. More than that, he brings them a smile and a dose of compassion.

He told *NBC News's* Bob Dotson that physicians don't do home visits anymore because they're "not efficient," but they give Dr. Richardson a better view of his patient as a whole person. And surprisingly, Medicare reimburses better for house calls than for office visits.

Dr. Richardson's compassion extends even further. Dotson writes, "Three nights a week, after all those house calls, Richardson teaches minority medical students who are struggling. He accepts no pay because in every one of those faces, he sees himself. He was the only black face in his medical school class. 'I was told many times [that my] grades aren't high enough to do this. But I did it.'"

I am the Lord who heals you. (Exodus 15:26)

Help me develop my talents so I can serve others, Creator.

With a Little Help From His Friends

Actor Howard McNear is best known for his comedic role as Floyd the Barber on *The Andy Griffith Show*. But several years into the show's run, his life took a serious turn when he had a stroke that rendered the left side of his body nearly paralyzed.

McNear was off the show for almost two years when Andy Griffith and writer/director Aaron Ruben came up with a story that they wanted to include him in. They called his home to see if he was willing and able to work. As recalled in Richard Kelly's book *The Andy Griffith Show*, McNear's wife Helen said of the offer, "It would be a godsend."

McNear's left side remained paralyzed, so they built him a special device that made it look like he was standing behind his barber chair. His mind had not been affected by the stroke, so McNear was still as funny as always. The writers brought him back for several more years, having him seated for his scenes or using his special stand. More than that, they helped a man who thought his career was over enjoy a job he loved once again.

Faith apart from works is barren. (James 2:20)

Guide our culture toward being more accommodating to those struggling with injury or disability, Jesus.

Death Row Chaplain

Earl Smith spent 27 years at San Quentin State Prison. But he wasn't there as an inmate; he served as a prison chaplain.

As a young man, Smith had gotten involved with drugs and gangs before choosing a better path. He therefore understands the backgrounds of the prison's inmates. He tells them to ask themselves, "Am I my crime?" because he knows that if they stop defining themselves by their crimes, they can start to rise above their wrongdoing.

In his memoir *Death Row Chaplain*, Smith writes, "Even if you think someone is his crime, God does not. He knows better. God doesn't have a checklist for forgiving us for our errors. He cares about one thing; that we ask Him sincerely for forgiveness through a relationship with Jesus Christ."

Smith makes sure to tell the inmates that God's forgiveness doesn't mean they'll escape from earthly justice. But it is a means of opening yourself to grace and moving forward in a positive way.

The Lord sets the prisoners free. (Psalm 146:7)

Guide the hearts of all sinners so they find redemption in You, Jesus.

This is Your Brain on Music

Can karaoke be good for society? In a way, yes, because music can have a positive cultural impact. Writing in *Living City* magazine, Emilie Christy highlights the reasons:

- **Music increases contact, coordination and cooperation.** "When performers try to synchronize music together with others, it produces positive feelings, and releases pleasure chemicals (endorphins) in the brain."

- **Music releases oxytocin.** "Experiments with amateur and professional singers have shown that oxytocin, a neuropeptide that plays an important role in forming bonds and trust among people, increases. This is true even when mothers sing lullabies to their infants."

- **Music increases cultural cohesion.** "Think of a national anthem played at a sports event or a lullaby passed on through generations. Each culture expresses its identity through some sort of music; studies find that connections are stronger among families and peer groups when they listen to music together."

I will sing to the Lord as long as I live. (Psalm 104:33)

Help us increase the harmony among all of humanity through the power of music, Lord.

The Class Trip That Wasn't

Senior class trips in high school fall into that "once-in-a-lifetime" category. They might run the gamut, from exotic locales to something right around the corner, but either way they spell the thrill of getting away from school for a day.

That's why the kids at Profile Junior-Senior High School in Bethlehem, New Hampshire, made an unusual amount of news when they planned their senior trip last year—and showed they had learned a lesson in compassion as well.

They voted to ditch the plans they had made for their senior trip and instead give the entire $8,000 they had raised to their principal, Courtney Vashaw, who is fighting a rare form of tissue cancer.

Vashaw has always taught students to be selfless, senior Ian Baker said in the *New York Post*, so it wasn't that difficult a decision. "She's just very caring, very selfless," he said, "and we wanted to be selfless too."

Let each of you look not to your own interests, but to the interests of others. Let the same mind be in you that was in Christ Jesus. (Philippians 2:4-5)

Nurture a spirit of selflessness in me, Divine Giver.

And Sew It Goes

Xavier Elliot, age 10, knows what it's like to be homeless. As reported by *ABC News*, he and his family were left displaced for nine years after his father, a disabled veteran, couldn't get the help he needed for post-traumatic stress disorder.

The Elliots now have a home in Phoenix, Arizona, and mom Stephanie "mends clothing for extra income." Xavier was keeping her company while she worked one day, and he told her that he "wanted to save his allowance to make clothes for homeless kids."

Stephanie said, "I think [homelessness] affected him a lot. Losing everything, having to start all over again, and seeing all the other kids in shelters — some of them were coming in from domestic violence and all they had were the clothes on their backs. So, he saw the need for it when we were in there."

When word of Xavier's mission spread, he started receiving lots of fabric donations. He now spends his free time at the family sewing machine using his skills to help others.

Make purses for yourselves that do not wear out, an unfailing treasure in heaven. (Luke 12:33)

Inspire the hearts of children to help others in need, Jesus.

God's Grace Got Them Through

Lud and Trudy Koci of West Bloomfield, Michigan, have lived quite a life. Married for nearly 60 years, they had eight children. And even though four of their children have died tragically, they remain steadfast in their faith.

"Their ability to endure the tragedies has nothing to do with their own volition and everything to do with God's grace," wrote Marge Fenelon in *Our Sunday Visitor*. "That, they say, was what got them through it all." Trudy added, "The Eucharist helped more than anything. If you really believe what the Eucharist is, how can it not help you?"

A family friend, Father Tim Whelan, explained that the Kocis are always donating their time, talent or treasure to some cause, adding: "Lud and Trudy have experienced more loss and grief in their lives than most people could imagine, but this hasn't made them bitter or resentful to God. They live the Paschal Mystery. In other words, they realize that real happiness isn't something you can find in this life. It is something that is shared with you in the next life by an all-loving God."

Be patient in suffering. (Romans 12:12)

When my heart breaks, Lord, bring me Your healing love.

Stop Comparing Yourself to Others

Though her two sons are now grown, blogger and author Lisa Hendey remembers what it was like being a young mother and how much pressure she put on herself to be perfect. This was especially true when it came time for church.

During a *Christopher Closeup* interview about her book *The Grace of Yes*, Hendey said, "[I was] the mom in the pew with the two screaming little kids. Then [I'd] look around and everyone else's family was beautifully dressed and they were all there 10 minutes early. I was just struggling to get there and keep both kids quiet in the pew. It was not pretty!

"I became frustrated by looking around and saying, 'Why aren't we like XYZ family?' And at a certain point I realized, 'Wow, God made our little domestic church just as it is. We're doing our very best to love Him, to know Him. And I have to stop this judging that I do of myself because that's not of God.'"

If you're doing your best to love God but judging yourself because you're not perfect, follow Hendey's lead. Don't let negativity become a stumbling block on your road to Him.

Judge with right judgment. (John 7:24)

Holy Spirit, guide my family's road to holiness.

From Complaint to Action

As he drove through Mineral Wells, Texas, Jim Rhodes noticed many vacant buildings, due to the shutdown of a local military base. "I always complain to God about things that bother me," says Rhodes. "So I asked Him, 'Why aren't these buildings being used to help the homeless?'"

Days later, a local newspaper reported that one of the buildings was available to any charitable organization that could put it to good use. Rhodes sent a letter to city officials with his idea, and they offered him the building.

With the help of donated services from plumbers, electricians and painters, Rhodes opened the New Haven Family Center. Since opening in 1993, the center has helped many families start a new life by providing clothes and food, as well as classes which develop skills needed for jobs.

What started as a complaint has become a better life for many. If something in your area bothers you, turn your complaint into action and make a difference.

Let your light shine before others, so that they may see your good works and give glory to your Father in heaven. (Matthew 5:16)

Lord, embolden me to put my faith into action.

A Far Away Reality

Jonathan Jackson and his band Enation aren't just concerned with making good music; they want to change the world for the better. For instance, the song *A Far Away Reality,* from their album *Radio Cinematic,* was inspired by the hellish situation for Christians being persecuted in Syria.

Several years ago, before the media began covering the war there, Jackson met an Orthodox Christian monk from Mount Athos in Greece, who told him about the conflict. Heartbroken by the suffering he was hearing about, Jackson wanted to express the victims' stories artistically to raise awareness.

In addition, Enation has a longstanding commitment to the organization Not For Sale, which goes into different countries to rescue and rehabilitate victims of human trafficking. Said Jackson's brother and Enation bandmate Richard Lee, "For us being artists, [we have] music available to help support them and play events for them. Anything we can do to help them fight human trafficking is something we're excited to be a part of."

I will bind up the injured, and I will strengthen the weak. (Ezekiel 34:16)

Remind me to help the persecuted in any way I can, Redeemer.

Actor Believes Faith is Force for Good

Before deciding to play Rev. Martin Luther King Jr. in the Christopher Award-winning movie *Selma*, actor David Oyelowo prayed about it. That's something he admits to doing before every job he takes, and it's something of a rarity in Hollywood for someone to speak so openly about his faith.

During The Family Entertainment & Faith-Based Summit in 2015, Oyelowo admitted that people sometimes tell him to cut down on the God talk. But the actor said, "It's just who I am, and I refuse to censor myself or marginalize something that I believe to be a force for good."

At the same time, Oyelowo believes his work is his ultimate statement about his faith: "I'm not interested in Bible-thumping or beating anyone over the head with the Gospel. But what I am interested in is talking about love, talking about goodness, talking about light in spite of a dark world, and letting that be reflected in my work. And if someone asks me, I will tell them who I am and what I believe, but the work is where I do my real talking."

Everyone...who acknowledges Me before others, I also will acknowledge. (Matthew 10:32)

May I never be ashamed of my faith in You, Jesus.

A Medical Mission of Hope

The late humorist and columnist Erma Bombeck supported the work of Esperança, an organization she described as "a handful of dreamers who thought they could run a boat up and down the Amazon dispensing medicine, love and life itself."

Actually Esperança (meaning *hope*) was founded in the 1970s by the late Franciscan priest-physician Luke Tupper. Father Tupper believed that medicine should be a holy profession, and that "each person we encounter should be treated with dignity and respect."

Esperança still attracts medical professionals and other volunteers to do immunizations, surgery and other medical and dental procedures on countless individuals in South America, Central America, Africa, and the United States. Their reward? The satisfaction of serving their brothers and sisters in need.

**Physicians...pray to the Lord that He grant them success in diagnosis and in healing.
(Sirach 38:12,13)**

May there always be physicians who imitate You, Divine Healer.

Who God Is Looking For

One of the songs on Matt Maher's album *Saints and Sinners* is called *Firelight*, and it was inspired by Mother Teresa's long struggle with darkness. The singer-songwriter was surprised that this was treated as a scandal by many news outlets.

He said, "I [wondered], 'What did you expect?' This brave woman goes to the poorest place on the planet and literally goes to help people die with dignity. I don't know anybody who wouldn't struggle with finding the presence of God."

Instead of turning people away from the faith, Maher believes Mother Teresa's witness in this sense should actually draw more people to the Church: "That struggle that [Mother Teresa] had, to me, I feel like we could do a whole ad campaign for vocations around it and say, 'This is who God's looking for. God's looking for people who don't have all the answers. God's looking for people who are willing to admit their own frailty.' But once again, I think that sometimes we're afraid of people seeing fully who we are. Yet God uses all of it for His glory."

You who have made me see many troubles and calamities will revive me again. (Psalm 71:20)

Help me to admit my own fears and weaknesses, Jesus.

Itzhak Perlman's Best Teacher

During her life, violin teacher Dorothy DeLay's students considered her the best teacher in the world. She was also their counselor and friend.

Probably the most famous of her former students is Itzhak Perlman. But DeLay did more than teach him how to play his chosen instrument; she helped build his self-confidence after polio had left him with severe disabilities.

Thirty years later, Perlman said of her, "She believed in me. There was a time when my parents and Miss DeLay were the only people in the world who believed I could have a career. The fact that I was disabled...People looked at me with distorted vision. And she never did. She was able to see."

To see and bring out the best in others is one of the most precious gifts one person can ever give another. Open your eyes—and praise the good you see around you.

Bear one another's burdens. (Galatians 6:2)

Giver of every talent and ability, help teachers and parents to encourage young people's gifts.

Angry Letter Leads to Life-Changing Work

During the early 1940s, Jane Harris worked as a writer in the world of advertising and celebrity publicity. A devout Catholic, she felt troubled by the fact that she was hobnobbing with actors while American servicemen were dying overseas.

Harris started seeking work that she felt was more in line with what God wanted her to do. One day, she read a newspaper ad with the headline: "Calling All Christopher Writers!" It encouraged writers who believed one person could change the world to contact a "James Keller."

Harris, who had lost her youthful idealism, felt outraged, and responded with her own letter: "Dear Mr. Keller: Change the WORLD? You have a lot of nerve to promote the idea." She then challenged him to tell her how exactly he proposed to do that.

A few days later, Harris received a letter from Father James Keller, founder of The Christophers, asking to meet with her. She didn't realize he was a priest and felt mortified by the error. However, Father Keller didn't mind. After their meeting, he hired Harris, making her one of the first Christopher employees.

Be...slow to anger. (James 1:19)

Thank You for turning mistakes into blessings, Father.

Giving Youth More Hope

Young adult novelist Joan Bauer earned one of her two Christopher Awards for the novel *Hope Was Here*. And hope is a virtue that she wants to impart to young people.

During an interview on *Christopher Closeup* about her latest book, entitled *Tell Me*, she said, "Kids have become very jaded. They've seen a lot of role models fall. They've seen difficulties in the world. And yet, one of the reasons that I love thinking about stories through the eyes of a young person is there's still this idealism. There's still this positive core."

Then she shared a personal story about the power of hope: "I got a letter about *Hope Was Here* [from] a girl who had leukemia. She got it when she was 12. She read *Hope Was Here* all during her chemotherapy. It was the only thing she read. And she said, 'Mrs. Bauer, I don't know what to tell you other than that I don't have leukemia anymore, and that book helped me. It just helped me.'...When [kids] find something that has hope, I think they really want to grab onto it. So let's give them more."

You, O Lord, are my hope. (Psalm 71:5)

Instead of dwelling on negativity, Lord, turn my mind to hope.

Guide to Contented Living

The famed German writer Goethe offered a list of nine requisites for contented living. They are as timely now as they were when he wrote them 200 years ago:

"Health enough to make work a pleasure. Wealth enough to support your needs. Strength enough to battle your difficulties and overcome them.

"Grace enough to confess your sins and forsake them. Patience enough to toil until some good is accomplished. Clarity enough to see some good in your neighbor.

"Love enough to move you to be useful to others. Faith enough to make real the things of God. Hope enough to remove all anxious fears concerning the future."

Goethe showed wisdom in these thoughts, perhaps especially in the use of the word "enough." Often we seek much more than we need when contentment and gratitude can come from having "enough."

There is great gain in godliness with contentment; for we brought nothing into the world, so that we can take nothing out of it. (1 Timothy 6:6-7)

Grace me with divine contentment, Jesus, for in having You, I do have everything.

This is for All Those People

When Michael Keaton won a Golden Globe award as Best Actor for the film *Birdman*, he delivered a memorable speech that highlighted the importance of family in his life:

"In the household in which I was raised, the themes were pretty simple: work hard, don't quit, be appreciative, be thankful, be respectful. Also, never whine ever, never complain, and, always, for crying out loud, keep a sense of humor.

"My name's Michael John Douglas, I'm from Forest Grove, Pennsylvania. I'm the son— seventh child—of George and Leona Douglas. And I don't ever remember a time when my father didn't work two jobs. When my mother wasn't saying the rosary or going to Mass or trying to take care of seven kids in a rundown farmhouse, she was volunteering at the Ohio Valley Hospital where I was born in the hallway. I've got six wonderful brothers and sisters...

"My best friend is kind, intelligent, funny, talented, considerate, thoughtful...He also happens to be my son, Sean. I love you with all my heart, buddy. This is for all those people."

Honor your father and your mother. (Exodus 20:12)

Thank You for the gift of family, Creator.

Dear Soldier

Eight-year-old Myles Eckert felt excited at having found a $20 bill outside a Cracker Barrel restaurant where he was going to eat with his family. At first, he thought he would buy a video game with the money. But after seeing a soldier inside, Eckert decided to give him the money instead. Wrapped around Eckert's twenty was this touching note:

"Dear Soldier—my dad was a soldier. He's in heaven now. I found this 20 dollars in the parking lot when we got here. We like to pay it forward in my family. It's your lucky day! Thank you for your service. Myles Eckert, a gold star kid."

Unfortunately, Myles's father, Army Sgt. Andy Eckert, died in Iraq only five months after his son was born. Although he doesn't remember his father, Myles still thinks about him a lot, and even visited his gravesite that very day.

As for the recipient of the $20, Lt. Col. Frank Dailey, he claims the boy's letter gave him a new "lifetime direction." He's already donated the $20, and plans to follow Myles's example and keep paying it forward.

Give, and it will be given to you. (Luke 6:38)

God, grant rest to the souls of all soldiers.

Heaven's Baseball Team

It was 1934 when the teens representing Springfield, Massachusetts' American Legion Post 21 baseball team headed to Gastonia, North Carolina, to play in the eastern sectional tournament. A win would have moved them one step closer to the national championship. But the team didn't win. In fact, they didn't even play.

The powers-that-be in Gastonia refused to let Post 21's lone African-American player, Bunny Taliaferro, into a hotel or onto their field. As reported by the website MassLive.com, "At this point, Taliaferro's teammates came to a quick and unanimous decision. They withdrew from the tournament, putting team togetherness ahead of a chance for a national championship."

The only remaining living player from that team is Tony King, who was celebrated for his courage by Springfield's mayor in 2014 on the 80th anniversary of the withdrawal. Mike Borecki, chairman of the committee that honored the team, said, "Tony King is our link to heaven's baseball team."

The Lord...loves righteous deeds. (Psalm 11:7)

Imbue me with the courage to pursue justice, Father.

Commandments to Get Along with People

Advice columnist Ann Landers once wrote "10 Commandments of How to Get Along with People." The inspirational newsletter *Apple Seeds* recently reprinted them:

1. "Keep skid chains on your tongue. Always say less than you think. Cultivate a low, persuasive voice. How you say it often counts more than what you say."

2. "Make promises sparingly and keep them faithfully, no matter what the cost."

3. "Never let an opportunity pass to say a kind and encouraging word to or about somebody."

4. "Be interested in others: their pursuits, their homes, and their families. Make merry with those who rejoice; with those who weep, mourn. Let everyone you meet, however humble, feel that you regard him or her as a person of importance."

5. "Be cheerful. Don't burden or depress those around you by dwelling on your aches and pains and small disappointments. Remember everyone is carrying some kind of burden."

We'll share the remaining commandments tomorrow.

Live peaceably with all. (Romans 12:18)

Help me choose my words wisely, Divine Word.

The Commandments Continue...

Today, the remaining tips from columnist Ann Landers' "10 Commandments of How to Get Along with People."

6. "Keep an open mind. Discuss, but don't argue. It is a mark of a superior mind to...disagree without being disagreeable."

7. "Let your virtues speak for themselves. Refuse to talk about the vices of others. Discourage gossip. It is a waste of valuable time and can be disruptive and hurtful."

8. "Take into consideration the feelings of others. Wit and humor at the expense of another is never worth the pain that may be inflicted."

9. "Pay no attention to ill-mannered remarks about you. Remember, the person who carried the message may not be the most accurate reporter in the world. Simply live so that nobody will believe him."

10. "Don't be anxious about the credit due you. Do your best and be patient. Forget about yourself and let others remember. Success is much sweeter that way."

Those with good sense are slow to anger. (Proverbs 19:11)

May we seek to create unity, not division, Prince of Peace.

Choosing What's Right

Most of us like to see ourselves as people of integrity. But do you ever wonder how you would act if put to the test?

Reuben Gonzales more than made the grade. He was in the final match of a major racquetball tournament and looking for his first professional win.

At match point in the final game, Gonzales made a super shot for the victory. The referee and the linesman called it good. But the almost-champion saw it differently.

Declaring that his shot had hit the floor before it skipped into the wall, he shook his opponent's hand and walked off the court.

Asked why he did it, Gonzales simply said, "It was the only thing I could do to maintain my integrity."

Honor and honesty can command a high price. That's why they are worth so much.

The Lord judges the peoples; judge me, O Lord, according to my righteousness and according to the integrity that is in me. (Psalm 7:8)

Thank You for the example of Your holy women and men of integrity and virtue, Creator.

The Vacuum Cleaner Salesman Cometh

For her son Dylan's 14th birthday, Jodie Greene surprised him with a special guest at his party: a vacuum cleaner salesman. That may sound unusual, but it's the best gift she could have gotten for Dylan, who has autism.

Since age two, Dylan has had a passion for vacuum cleaners, especially the Cleveland-based Kirby brand. When spending time online, he would watch videos about their products.

Greene wrote a letter to Kirby headquarters asking if one of their salesmen could come to their Chesterfield County, Virginia home and do a demo at Dylan's party. They happily obliged, sending Al Archie, a 25-year veteran of the company.

Dylan was thrilled by the demonstration, but ecstatic when he got an even bigger surprise. Archie gave the teen a brand new Kirby vacuum. "There was not a dry eye in the house," recalled Greene. Despite the fact that Kirbys are not cheap, Archie explained that he simply wanted to do something special for Dylan. Greene joked, "I'm going to have the cleanest carpets in Chesterfield County."

You have shown me great kindness. (Genesis 19:19)

Help me go the extra mile to make someone's day, Lord.

The Business of Dreams

E. Yip Harburg is a name you might not recognize, but the world sings his songs. Isidor Hochberg, son of Russian immigrants, was born in New York in 1896. When he married he changed his name, but never forgot who he was.

Like Irving Berlin, another giant among Broadway songwriters, Harburg grew up poor. He made money, but lost it in the stock market crash of 1929. "When I lost my possessions, I found my creativity. I gave up the dream of business and went into the business of dreams."

His songs are full of heart. "In a lot of songs I write, I cry. I write with what they call in Yiddish *gederim*—it means the very vitals of your being. I feel everything." He put his feelings into classics like "Brother, Can You Spare a Dime?" and "Somewhere Over the Rainbow."

Harburg believed that if you could control the songs of a nation, you didn't need to care about its laws. His upbeat songs also reflected his belief that "If (a song) gives me courage, it'll give others courage."

The Lord is my strength. (Exodus 15:1)

Help me to courageously live out my dreams, Lord.

The Wisdom That Comes with Age

Older workers around the country are defying modern stereotypes about age by seeking and holding jobs beyond the time when many look to retire. Reporting for *The New York Times*, Kerry Hannon offers Mary Doan, the former chief executive of the advertising agency Saatchi & Saatchi's San Francisco office, as a perfect example.

Doan earns a living by taking on short-term marketing and development projects that last anywhere from a few months to a year. She says, "I'm just happy to roll up my sleeves and be engaged."

Hannon notes that smaller organizations, such as nonprofits and niche educational programs, tend to welcome the wisdom that comes with age. She highlights the story of James S. Kunen, a former director of corporate communications at Time Warner, who now teaches English as a second language in Queens.

He says, "At this age and stage of my life, working with highly motivated immigrants gives me a sense of purpose and engagement with the world...Going to work is spending time with friends. I feel appreciated."

The price of wisdom is above pearls.
(Job 28:18)

Lord, help us to respect our elders and value their wisdom.

Eighteen States and Counting

Kara Jackson's mission began when she and her mother Christina said a prayer before dropping a letter in a mailbox. Two days later, both their prayer and letter were answered.

Kara, a 16-year-old with Down Syndrome, became an altar server at age nine in Holy Family Parish in Middletown, Ohio. She always performed her duties exceptionally well and soon got the idea that she'd like to serve at Mass in all 50 states.

As reported by *Catholic News Service*, her first attempt was to contact Father Kevin Morris, pastor of St. Mary Church in Richmond, Indiana, by mail to see if he would let her serve there. He answered "yes," and so began Jackson's unique journey.

So far, she has visited 18 states, impressing priests and parishioners alike. Archbishop Joseph E. Kurtz of Louisville, Kentucky—whose late brother had Down Syndrome—said, "Kara's beautiful personality and unique gifts reinforced our church's teachings about the dignity of every human being."

The plans of the diligent lead surely to abundance. (Proverbs 21:5)

Teach the world, Father, that sometimes disabilities are simply different abilities.

Newtown and the Sandy Ground Project

It's been four long years since that awful day in December 2012 when 26 people—20 first-graders and six educators—were killed in the shooting at Sandy Hook Elementary School in Newtown, Connecticut. For most people, that day seems as if it were only yesterday. And yet, one memorial marking the somber event has come full circle, and thousands of children are its beneficiaries.

In September of 2014, the last of 26 playgrounds, one named for each victim of the shooting, was dedicated in Watertown, Connecticut, honoring Sandy Hook's heroic principal, Dawn Hochsprung. The playgrounds were all built in New York, New Jersey and Connecticut, states most affected by Hurricane Sandy, which struck a few weeks before the tragic events in Newtown. All were constructed under the Sandy Ground Project, established for that purpose.

All the children of Watertown will benefit from the playground, including some special guests—the grandchildren of Principal Hochsprung.

You have turned my mourning into dancing. (Psalm 30:11)

Help us to bring hope out of tragedy, Divine Healer.

The Atheist and the Bear

Heard the one about the atheist and the bear? If not, you're in for a treat. Father Joe Breighner tells it in his regular column in the Baltimore *Catholic Review*, and it goes like this:

An atheist was walking through the woods one day, enjoying himself, when suddenly he came across a bear. The atheist began to run, and the bear ran after him. Then the atheist tripped and fell, and the bear landed right on top of him.

"Oh God, save me!" the atheist hollered, and sure enough, God's voice was right there. "All these years you've denied My existence," the voice said, "and now you want Me to save you?"

"Yep, that would be hypocritical," the atheist conceded. "Why don't You just make the bear a Christian?" he said. "That should solve everything."

"So be it," God's voice answered.

The bear moved off the atheist, knelt, and folded his paws in prayer, saying, "Bless us O Lord, and these thy gifts, which we are about to receive…"

God has brought laughter for me; everyone who hears will laugh with me. (Genesis 21:6)

Instill me with a good sense of humor, Heavenly Father.

Money Matters For Children

Do your children crave the latest tech gadgets, coolest sneakers, or fanciest set of headphones? In our consumer society a child's wish list can be long.

What's an adult to do? You can set limits, even if you're comfortable financially. In her "Young Urban Moms" column for the *Manhattan Times*, Carolina Pichardo offers suggestions:

- **Check yourself.** What do your spending habits convey to your children? Adults aren't immune from wanting the latest goodies that suggest their status, wealth or achievement.

- **Talk it out.** Your goal is to help your child make wise spending/savings decisions. Your approach will change depending upon their ages. For instance, tell them what they can spend their allowance on or why you look for sales.

- **Terms and Conditions.** Teach your children about money, budgets, bank accounts, assets, debt, financial planning.

- **C'mon, splurge a little.** An occasional impulse buy "is no sin." But remember to invest in experiences, too.

Wealth hastily gotten will dwindle, but those who gather little by little will increase it. (Proverbs 13:11)

Inspire us, Holy Spirit, to build and use our assets wisely.

The Road Not Taken

TV host Mike Rowe created a foundation that offers scholarships to people who want to learn a trade. Several companies financially supported his efforts, so he took to Facebook to thank them and explain his devotion to the cause:

"The many hundreds of franchisees that comprise Benjamin Franklin Plumbing, Mister Sparky, and One-Hour Heating and Air Conditioning are looking to hire about 2,000 qualified technicians. Specifically, they're looking for electricians, plumbers, and HVAC professionals...

"All of these trades offer more than a job and a shot at a six-figure salary; they offer a long-term career that can easily evolve into a small business. The fact that so few people are currently trained to do the available work is something close to a crime, and the fact that more people aren't lining up to get the necessary training is preposterous. I'm pleased to help spread the word about these and other opportunities available within these specific companies...[I hope they] inspire more people to master a useful skill."

The hand of the diligent makes rich.
(Proverbs 10:4)

Lead the unemployed toward meaningful work, Creator.

The Unexpected Family Reunion

La-Sonya Mitchell-Clark of Youngstown, Ohio, was adopted as a baby, but wanted to reconnect with her birth mother. After requesting records recently made available by the Ohio Department of Health, she found out that her mother's name is Francine Simmons.

Mitchell-Clark looked Simmons up on Facebook only to discover that her mother works for the same company where she works!

As reported by *CBS News*, Simmons always wanted to find the daughter she gave away when she gave birth at age 15. She recalls holding Mitchell-Clark briefly before authorities took her off to a group home.

Now, Mitchell-Clark has connected with three sisters she never knew she had as well. "It's just amazing," said one sister, "that all this time we're thinking about her and trying to find her—and she was trying to find us, too." Simmons expressed great joy over finding her daughter, saying, "Now, we've got a bigger extended family where we can just be together."

Clothe yourselves with love, which binds everything together in perfect harmony. (Colossians 3:14)

Lord, help us to repair and maintain our family bonds.

Fairy Tales and Deeper Truths

Author Nicole Lataif and illustrator Katy Betz may have won a 2015 Christopher Award for their children's book *I Forgive You*, but its appeal can extend beyond its intended audience. In a way, the book is appropriate for adults as well who may not have time to read lengthy explorations of the topic.

Through simple-but-meaningful words—and illustrations that convey joy, humor and sorrow, Lataif and Betz capture the essence of learning to forgive others, choosing to ask forgiveness from those you've hurt and from God, and learning to forgive without letting people walk all over you.

Betz appreciates the book's cross-generational appeal as well, citing a favorite quote by author C.S. Lewis: "Someday you will be old enough to start reading fairy tales again." She explained on *Christopher Closeup* that adults often dismiss so-called children's stories because they think they're not complex: "But that's the beauty of fairy tales and picture books because the metaphors do hold a deeper truth."

These things God has revealed to us through the Spirit; for the Spirit searches everything. (1 Corinthians 2:10)

Reveal Yourself to me, Lord, in unexpected ways.

Ex-Cons and Busy Bees

Brenda Palms Barber converted a patch of weeds at the end of a Chicago airport runway into a honey business that turns ex-convicts into busy bees.

As reported by *NBC News's* Bob Dotson, 80 percent of the men living in North Lawndale have been in jail, so it's difficult for them to find a job of any kind. Seeing that this was a problem in need of a solution, Barber got a grant from the Illinois Corrections Department, hired the 83-year-old former president of the Illinois Beekeepers Association to train new employees, and started a company called Sweet Beginnings.

Most of the former prison inmates work there for two-and-a-half months before searching for employment elsewhere with Barber's full support. She said, "Working with beehives shifts the business interview from 'What did you do bad that landed you in prison' to 'What's it like to work with bees?'"

So far, Sweet Beginnings has provided 360 jobs, and its honey brings in $300,000 a year. Said ex-convict James White about the work, "I found peace."

Remember those who are in prison. (Hebrews 13:3)

Send former prisoners opportunities to change their lives, Forgiving Father.

A Beautiful and Generous Gesture

In April and May of 2015, St. Catherine of Siena Church in Mississauga, Canada, was repeatedly vandalized. The altar was broken, a statue of Jesus was desecrated with black paint, and graffiti covered the walls of the church's school, reported the *Toronto Star*. Police caught the mentally ill perpetrator, but the damage was already done and would cost $10,000 to repair.

When word spread, the church received help from an unexpected source. Hamid Slimi, imam of a nearby mosque, paid a visit to see the damage himself. He called it "pure injustice," and appealed to his own congregation to help St. Catherine's financially. They contributed a total of $5,000.

Father Camillo Lando, the pastor of St. Catherine's, felt grateful. He said, "I will tell my congregation that it was a really beautiful and generous gesture on their part. And also, it's an act of confidence and understanding. We are walking together in this community. We keep our faith, and we have to honor and respect people of other faiths."

As God's chosen ones, holy and beloved, clothe yourselves with compassion. (Colossians 3:12)

Inspire us to respect people of other faiths, Creator of All.

Talents to Share

On the website TheMighty.com, Sharon Belott reports on a growing trend towards inclusion of those with disabilities in the workforce. She notes that Arc of San Francisco, a community-based support group for those with disabilities, has worked with the city's tech sector to find training and employment for over 700 people with corporate giants like Salesforce and Twitter.

Arc of Indiana is building a Courtyard by Marriott that will house a postsecondary institute for hospitality, food services and healthcare. And Arc of Jefferson County in Alabama has been starting businesses to employ those with behavioral issues.

"Everyone is striving to build an inclusive culture," said Jill Houghton, Executive Director of the United States Business Leadership Network, a group that explores the intersection between capitalism and disability. "As companies are on that journey, we see how it drives innovation, morale, better customer service, better problem solving—everything increases for the better as a result of inclusion."

Do to others as you would have them do to you. (Luke 6:31)

Lord, guide us to see the talents in all Your children.

Rosh Hashanah: The Basics

Eric Levenson gets asked the same questions every year by his non-Jewish friends when the Jewish High Holidays come around, so in 2014, he answered several of them on Boston.com.

The first High Holiday is Rosh Hashanah, a two-day celebration of the Jewish new year. The date changes because it's determined by a lunar calendar, not the Gregorian calendar, which is used by most of the world. This calendar also defines each day as starting at sunset instead of midnight. "That's why Rosh Hashanah and Yom Kippur start at night," Levenson said.

On Rosh Hashanah, Jewish people "go to synagogue, reflect on life, and spend time with family." Some families cook big beef briskets or indulge in eating apples and honey "to symbolize the hope that the new year will be sweet…There's also the shofar, a loud, bugle-like noisemaker made from a ram's horn. The shofar is like a call to attention, and everyone in synagogue stands and gets quiet to hear the call."

Tomorrow, the basics of Yom Kippur.

You shall observe…a holy convocation commemorated with trumpet blasts. (Leviticus 23:24)

May we always hear and heed Your call, Heavenly Father.

Yom Kippur: The Basics

On Boston.com, writer Eric Levenson explained the basics of the Jewish High Holidays—Rosh Hashanah and Yom Kippur—to those unfamiliar with them. While Rosh Hashanah is a festive new year celebration, Yom Kippur, which follows 10 days later, is a more solemn occasion—at least at first.

"On Yom Kippur," wrote Levenson, "you don't drink or eat anything for a whole day. You're encouraged to reflect on your own faults, apologize to people you've wronged, and generally think about all the things you said you would do but failed to do over the past year.

"Yom Kippur—or the Day of Atonement, as it's sometimes called—isn't supposed to be a fun holiday. It's meant to be meaningful and a way to think about how to be a better person for the coming year. There is a big feast at the end of the fast, with all the food you could ever imagine, (and which you've in fact been imagining the entire, hunger-filled day). Starve yourself for a day and that chocolate cake is twice as delicious."

The tenth day of this seventh month is the day of atonement. (Leviticus 23:26)

Help me acknowledge and atone for my sins, Lord.

Everything is Grace

St. Thérèse of Lisieux is a much-beloved saint because of her simple yet profound approach to loving God and doing His will. Yet from a worldly perspective, she did nothing significant with her life. At age 15, she entered the convent where she died of tuberculosis at age 24.

On her deathbed, she uttered the words, "Everything is grace," which reflected her philosophy that even life's struggles had purpose in the greater scheme of things. Singer Matt Maher is an admirer of St. Thérèse, and wrote a song inspired by her called *Everything is Grace*.

During a *Christopher Closeup* interview, he said, "Thérèse was such a profound example for young people who feel tempted to complain of an insignificant life because she found great significance [even in] the storms...A lot of those valleys that we walk through can become profound places of transformation where we're actually brought closer to God. There is an opportunity in everything to receive grace for the journey and for life, and to love people no matter how difficult things may seem."

God...gives grace to the humble. (James 4:6)

Instill me with the vision to see Your grace, Lord.

A Lesson from People with Disabilities

Though he writes thrillers, novelist Dean Koontz uses his stories to affirm life, especially in his treatment of characters with disabilities. That stems from his and his wife Gerda's 30-year involvement with the charity Canine Companions for Independence, which provides assistance dogs to adults and children with disabilities.

Koontz has personally met many of these people and has learned quite a bit from them. During a *Christopher Closeup* interview, he said, "The older I get, the more internal beauty seems to matter. I've met hundreds of severely disabled people, but in all these years, I haven't heard one of them complain. I haven't heard one of them whine about anything in their lives—and they have much more to struggle with than other people do.

"It starts making you think, 'What strength or quality of character is it that this person has [that they've] become so much more pleasant to be around than many people with all their faculties?' I think that unfortunately, because of your disability, you learn humility, which a lot of us take our whole lives to learn and discover."

Humility goes before honor. (Proverbs 15:33)

Make me humble enough to appreciate my blessings, Lord.

God Shows the Way

Three men, all recovering alcoholics, one day happened upon a country inn that advertised home-made pumpkin pie. They engaged their waitress in conversation and mentioned their struggles to her. She felt a little nervous when she asked what their drink order would be, but they all simply drank colas. But when it was time for dessert, she informed them that the kitchen had just run out of pie.

Seeing their disappointment, she reappeared a few minutes later with three pieces. She had told the cooks that these three men just had to have that pumpkin pie. The cooks then offered the slices they had put aside for themselves.

"I'm in AA too," the waitress told the three strangers. "It's pretty tough right now. All day I've been praying for strength. Then out of nowhere you guys appear and I hear you talking. Just when I was feeling lost, you guys found me."

The Lord works in mysterious ways, indeed.

God sent me to heal you...I am Raphael, one of the seven angels who stand...before...the Lord. (Tobit 12:14,15)

Father, may I strive to be a source of encouragement to others.

A Very Fine Flying Cow

Theodore Geisel's art teacher told him he couldn't draw, and publishers said he couldn't write. His Dartmouth College fraternity voted him least likely to succeed. As a student at Oxford University in England, he was often bored with lectures.

Then, Geisel received one sentence of praise which was enough to motivate him to continue his dream of becoming a writer and educator.

That sentence was uttered during a class at Oxford when Geisel drew a cow with wings, an acrobat's body, and a mischievous expression. "That's a very fine flying cow," said Helen Palmer, a doctoral student in English literature.

Geisel—now better known as Dr. Seuss—bolstered by support from Palmer, whom he later married, became the author of such children's books as *The Cat in the Hat* (500,000 copies sold in its first year in print). His story demonstrates how far you can go with a little talent—and encouragement.

Do not judge. (Matthew 7:1)

Father, give me the vision to see the potential in others, so I can encourage them to be the people You want them to be.

Kelly Anne's Legacy of Hope

In 1976, Joe and Peggy Dolan experienced the worst pain a parent can endure: the loss of their six-year-old daughter Kelly Anne from leukemia. The years leading up to her death left the Dolans' lives filled with hospital visits, mounting bills, and exhaustion. Yet they were able to keep themselves afloat.

The other families they met with sick children weren't always so lucky. Some lost their jobs or homes due to exorbitant medical bills. Others had to decide between paying a doctor's co-pay or the utility bill.

The best way to honor Kelly Anne's memory, decided the Dolans, was to establish a fund in her name that would be a lifeline for these struggling families.

Celebrating its 40th anniversary in 2016, The Kelly Anne Dolan Memorial Fund provides financial support for families "caring for children with serious illnesses, disabilities, and injuries" that are not covered by insurance. Their mission has brought hope, love, and support to more than 23,000 families since 1976, cementing a little girl's life-changing legacy.

Love is strong as death. (Song of Solomon 8:6)

Guide me through the darkness of tragedy, Lord, with a light that I can share with others.

A Life of Greatness

As a football player with a $37 million contract with the St. Louis Rams, Jason Brown was living the dream. That's why it was surprising when he walked away from it all.

When the Rams didn't renew Brown's contract in 2012, other teams expressed interest in signing him, but he rejected them. Why? Because he decided to become a farmer, despite having never farmed in his life.

His main goal was to feed the hungry, and he believed farming was the best way to do that. As he told *CBS News's* Steve Hartman, "When I think about a life of greatness, I think about a life of service."

Through watching Youtube videos and getting advice from local farmers in Louisburg, North Carolina, Brown brought his dream to fruition. He started by growing sweet potatoes on five acres out of 1,000, and donated the first fruits to food pantries in his area. He plans to keep growing his farm year by year.

Brown considers himself successful "in God's eyes," and concludes, "Love is the most wonderful currency that you can give anyone."

The first fruits...shall be yours. (Numbers 18:13)

Help me define success by Your standards, Lord, not the world's.

Crusader for Safety

Nadine Milford went into shock when her daughter Melanie and three little grandchildren were killed by a drunk driver. In her pain, she asked God what to do.

The bereaved woman decided to fight for stricter laws and penalties for driving while intoxicated. And she didn't let the fact that she had no advocacy experience stop her. With friends and supporters, she traveled 60 miles a day to lobby state legislators—and she was successful.

New Mexico's attorney general said that "the accident galvanized public opinion in a way that we had never seen before...Nadine organized a grassroots campaign that made a real impact."

Milford admits that she often wanted to go home and just "pull the sheets over my head." But above anything else, she wanted the deaths of her daughter and grandchildren to have meaning. With her help, they do.

Is it lawful to do good or to do harm...to save life or to kill? (Mark 3:4)

Wisdom of the Father, inspire our efforts to protect the precious life You have given us.

Style versus Substance

On the CBS TV series *Madam Secretary*, fictional Secretary of State Elizabeth McCord does her best to solve the world's problems. The show's pilot episode also managed to criticize the media's shallow coverage of politics.

The main storyline involved two American teens who traveled to Syria to be freedom fighters of sorts, promptly getting themselves arrested and sentenced to death for being American spies. In an effort dubbed "Operation Stupid Kids," McCord devises a secret plan to rescue them. Then she discovers the story may become front-page news, putting her plans in jeopardy.

How, she wonders, can she give the press a bigger story to cover that will distract them? She then remembers that the press is obsessed with her lack of fashion sense, so she decides to undergo a makeover. McCord's ploy works, leaving reporters fawning all over her, and literally choosing style over substance.

When you read or watch political news, be aware of when you're being fed style over substance—and contact your local media outlets asking them to raise their standards.

Righteousness exalts a nation. (Proverbs 14:34)

Bless the media with the wisdom to report truth, Father.

Praise vs. Criticism

There is an old adage which contains a wealth of wisdom: "Praise publicly, criticize privately." Good idea, whether you are a CEO or a teacher or a parent.

People like to be praised, and they like it even better if it is done in public. On the other hand, nobody enjoys having their mistakes broadcast aloud. It is a wise person who knows how to praise or blame.

On the whole, it's always better to build people up than tear them down. A pat on the back goes a lot further than a figurative kick in the pants. You get the best from others if you give your best.

If you have to criticize, do it in private, without the heat of anger. Criticism is meant to help, not hurt. Criticism need not be a negative thing. It all depends on how gently it is given— and how graciously it is received.

Let another praise you, and not your own mouth. (Proverbs 27:2)

Grant me the wisdom to always speak with kindness and tact, Holy Spirit.

The Man with the Golden Arm

Until the mid-1960s, thousands of babies died in Australia every year and doctors didn't know why. Jemma Falkenmire, from the Australian Red Cross Blood Service, told *CNN*, "Women were having numerous miscarriages and babies were being born with brain damage."

The cause was finally determined to be rhesus disease, which causes a pregnant woman's blood cells to attack the blood cells of her unborn child.

Enter James Harrison, who became a regular blood donor because he had received many units of blood himself when he needed surgery as a teen. His blood, it was discovered, contained an unusual antibody that could combat rhesus disease. Doctors used it to create a vaccine for at-risk women.

In order to keep that healing process going, Harrison has donated his blood almost every week for the past 60 years, resulting in two million babies' lives being saved. He has been dubbed "The Man with the Golden Arm" and is considered a national hero.

**The life of the flesh is in the blood.
(Leviticus 17:11)**

Bless all blood donors, Jesus, for their life-saving efforts.

Interfaith Collaboration Feeds the Hungry

You wouldn't expect residents of a rich county in upstate New York to be suffering from poverty, but that is the case for many senior citizens in Getzville. As a result, Catholic and Jewish groups have joined forces to bring food to those in need.

As reported by *The Buffalo News*, the Town Square Association converted a local building into a food pantry, then asked Temple Beth Zion to collect food donations from its congregation as a good deed prior to Yom Kippur. Members of the temple did so, and agreed to volunteer at the site.

More help was needed so they contacted Catholic Charities, which has a proven track record in managing food pantries. Eileen Nowak, director of parish outreach and advocacy for Catholic Charities, said, "It's a wonderful collaboration, which I don't think has really been done to this extent before."

Adds Gary Pokras, senior rabbi at Temple Beth Zion, "We have an obligation to do everything that we can…towards helping to realize the vision ultimately for what creation can be. The best way we do that is by helping each other."

He will feed his flock like a shepherd. (Isaiah 40:11)

Guide us toward linking arms with our brothers and sisters in faith, Father.

Pastor Tends an Unwanted Flock

In 2011, University of Southern California filmmaking student Brian Ivie read a story in the *Los Angeles Times* titled "South Korean Pastor Tends an Unwanted Flock."

It shared the actions of Pastor Jong-rak Lee, who had built a drop box for unwanted babies into his home and church. The reason was that many babies born disabled or to single mothers in Seoul, South Korea, were abandoned on the streets to die because the culture often views these things as shameful.

With a heart full of love for these children, Pastor Lee and his wife started taking them in, finding them homes, and even adopted 18 themselves. To date, over 600 babies have been saved because of Pastor Lee's efforts.

Though Ivie had never considered making a documentary, he raised money, assembled a crew, and traveled to South Korea to temporarily live at Pastor Lee's Ju-sarang (God's Love) Community Church, to capture the essence of what they do there.

More of the story tomorrow.

Rescue the weak and the needy. (Psalm 82:4)

Open people's hearts toward loving children and adults with disabilities, Father.

The Weak Shame the Strong

This ministry wasn't Pastor Lee's first exposure to disabled children. His own son, Eun-man, was born with cerebral palsy and with a cyst that blocked blood flow to his brain, leaving him permanently brain-damaged.

At first, Pastor Lee wondered why God wouldn't give him a healthy child. Then he came to a realization. Ivie explained, "God put Eun-man on earth in this way because the weak shame the strong. He uses people that are weak and helpless to change the world."

Eun-man is 29 years old and he's lived his entire life in bed with twisted limbs, unable to speak. Despite this, Pastor Lee and his staff call Eun-man's room "the happy room." Why?

Ivie said, "Even though he lays on his back and has severe brain damage, he has one of the best smiles on planet Earth. So for Pastor Lee, [calling it the happy room] is a rebellion against what society would call satisfaction or happiness."

The conclusion of the story tomorrow.

You are the God of the lowly, helper of the oppressed, upholder of the weak. (Judith 9:11)

Expand my outlook on what constitutes true happiness, Creator.

Don't Reject Happy Endings

Brian Ivie completed his documentary about Pastor Lee and called it *The Drop Box*. It received positive reviews wherever it was shown. Now, Ivie hopes to continue his filmmaking journey. During an interview on *Christopher Closeup*, he said, "I call film school my seminary because it taught me how to tell stories. Now I want to tell stories about what God is like."

He also hopes to incorporate the lessons he learned making *The Drop Box* into his career. He said, "I think people have an authenticity meter, so when they see a movie and it doesn't feel like it's burst out of pain, immediately it's fake. That's why I try to tell stories that have my heart broken all over them.

"We're all made in the image of God and we all go through this world and think, 'This isn't how it should be. It shouldn't be hopeless or a mess. I shouldn't be broken. Maybe there's an answer for that.' That's why I don't reject happy endings, because they're not naive. It's what we all desire because we still have the imprint of how God always wanted it to be."

I am making all things new. (Revelations 21:5)

Bless filmmakers with talent and faith, Divine Creator.

A Life of Faith and Action

Jesus called you to live a life consisting of both faith and action, to live a life in which you love God and neighbor.

St. Teresa of Avila, the 16th-century mystic, had a full understanding of this ideal when she wrote the following reflection:

"Christ has no body now, but yours. No hands, no feet on earth, but yours. Yours are the eyes through which Christ looks compassion into the world. Yours are the feet with which Christ walks to do good. Yours are the hands with which Christ blesses the world.

"Let nothing trouble you, let nothing frighten you. All things are passing; God never changes. Patience obtains all things. He who possesses God lacks nothing: God alone suffices."

You shall love the Lord your God with all your heart, and with all your soul, and with all your strength, and with all your mind; and your neighbor as yourself. (Luke 10:27)

Grant me the grace, Jesus, to model a life devoted to You, and lead others closer to Your Sacred Heart.

Hockey's Quiet Hero

Sixty-seven-year-old Hockey Hall of Famer Bobby Orr accomplished some legendary feats on the ice with the Boston Bruins, but it's the things he's quietly done in his personal life that earn him true hero status.

Orr never sought publicity for these acts of kindness. In fact, he grew angry if someone talked about them. Nevertheless, several recipients of his generosity opted to share their memories with the *Boston Globe*.

Derek Sanderson, Orr's former teammate, recalled how Orr rescued him from an addiction to drugs and alcohol, sticking with him through 12 relapses and paying for every treatment. And when Bruins trainer John Forristall, with whom Orr lived early in his career, was diagnosed with terminal brain cancer, Orr took him in and cared for him until he passed away.

Those are just two instances of many, but they serve as a testament to a sports figure who exemplifies character.

When you give alms, do not let your left hand know what your right hand is doing, so that your alms may be done in secret; and your Father who sees in secret will reward you. (Matthew 6:3-4)

Guide me in practicing anonymous acts of kindness, Lord.

Go Boldly

Driving along a highway in Grand Rapids, Michigan, photographer Bri Luginbill saw many Botox ads featuring the tagline: "Go confidently." But how confident could a woman be, she thought, if she felt she had to alter every physical feature of her body?

Luginbill decided to combat the media's initiative for plastic surgery with a better one of her own. Thus, the "Go Boldly" campaign was born. Luginbill's pictures highlight women with all different body shapes and types. Among the young ladies featured in her portraits is 21-year-old Christina Parilla, a college student who had struggled with body issues.

"I am not a model, and a lot of times I feel weird just standing there and having someone take a bunch of pictures," Parilla told *The Florida Catholic*. "What I loved most about being photographed by Bri is how comfortable she made me feel...I think women should love their bodies because it's the only one they are going to get. Your eyes, nose, curves—those are all things that make you, you."

How beautiful you are, my love.
(Song of Solomon 4:1)

Jesus, help us to embrace our inner and outer beauty.

Parenting Pointers

Parenting is a tough yet rewarding vocation. Dr. Tim Elmore, author of *Generation iY: Our Last Chance to Save Their Future*, offers some simple but effective parenting tips:

- Talk to your children about issues you wish your parents would have discussed with you.
- Outline the consequences for any potential wrongdoing.
- Help your kids discover and utilize their talents.
- Set up projects that require patience and perseverance.
- Teach your children how to balance priorities.
- Simulate adult tasks, like paying bills; it's never too early.
- Introduce them to potential mentors/friends.
- Help your kids envision a bright future—and do what you can to assist them in getting there.
- Celebrate any progress your children make towards gaining their independence.

Children, obey your parents...for this is right. (Ephesians 6:1)

Heavenly Father, may all mothers and fathers look to You as the epitome of parenthood.

The Trash Truck Driver's Mission

In 2007, Arnold Harvey, a sanitation driver working in Silver Spring, Maryland, began to notice more people sleeping on the streets of his overnight route. He and his wife, Theresa, decided to collect food and blankets to hand out to those in need.

In a *Good Morning America* segment on their story, the Harveys can be seen driving around in the early morning hours to deliver what they call "love bags." At one point, Arnold approaches a man lying on a bench and sets a bag beside him, saying, "I'm gonna leave you this bag, man." Then he asks, "You know who I am?"

The man responds, "You're the trash truck driver." Arnold looks up with a big smile and says, "That's right. God bless you, buddy," and continues on his way.

The Harveys' ministry led them to start a food bank run out of a rented warehouse. Theresa says, "The reason we're here is the passion of God, the love of people." And Arnold adds, "As long as I know there's somebody out here, it's hard to go home, sit at a table, eat a meal. That's it."

For I was hungry and you gave Me food. (Matthew 25:35)

Lord, help us to see Your face in the poor and hungry.

Prescription for Health

People who eat fruit tend to be healthier than those who don't, reported a new Oxford University study of nearly half a million Chinese people from 10 different rural and urban areas.

Reporting on the topic for the website Mic.com, Erin Brodwin notes that participants were lumped into categories based on how much fruit they eat, ranging from "never" to "daily." Over a seven-year period, 20,000 developed heart disease and another 20,000 had strokes. "But people who ate fruit every day," Brodwin writes, "were far less likely to succumb to disease and death."

Health benefits from fruit can be derived from blueberries, strawberries, apples, oranges, and more. Daily fruit eaters in the study tended to consume one and a half portions each day and had a 25-to-40% lower risk of cardiovascular disease, and a 25-to-40% lower risk of stroke. Brodwin concludes, "Next time you pack a lunch, toss a piece of fruit in the bag. It might mean a lot more lunches down the road."

Your body is a temple of the Holy Spirit... Therefore glorify God in your body. (1 Corinthians 6:19-20)

Lord, may we respect our bodies and cultivate good health.

A Soldier Gets His Due

When Ben Davis first arrived at West Point he was greeted—by silence. It was the same the next day, and the day after that. The same all four years, in fact; he roomed alone and no one among his fellow cadets befriended him. Davis had been "shunned," in cadet parlance; he was ostracized.

Benjamin O. Davis Jr. wouldn't buckle. He graduated 35th in a class of 276, and rose in the ranks. He kept rising, in fact, until he reached the rank of lieutenant general, and President Bill Clinton added the fourth star on his retirement.

Davis started at West Point in 1932, the first black cadet of the 20th century. His fellow cadets didn't want him there, and he was just as determined to stay. And now, in 2015, they're going to name a new building at the Point for him, a rare honor previously reserved for people named Eisenhower or MacArthur.

"He is the epitome of what we want at a time when we didn't know what 'right' looked like," said the colonel who headed the naming committee. "It's our chance to acknowledge one of our greatest graduates."

Suffering produces endurance. (Romans 5:3)

May I judge people by their character, not color, Lord.

Teen's CPR Training Saves a Life

Call it instinct, call it training, call it whatever—but Ashley Giron of Brooklyn came through when it counted, in a way that few 18-year-olds are called on to do.

What the teenager did, as reported in the *New York Post*, was save the life of a two-year-old girl who had fallen from a third-floor apartment window.

Giron had had lessons in CPR, and she called on them when little Nygeana Civil plummeted from her apartment window on a warm spring evening last year. "At first, the baby wasn't breathing," Giron said, "but I knew I had to give her the standard CPR. Suddenly, the child started breathing. I was just shaken up."

A window guard was in place, but Nygeana managed to crawl past it. EMTs took her to a hospital, where she was in stable condition with serious injuries. "It just seems like a horrible tragedy," a police source said. "It could have been a lot worse."

Be dressed for action. (Luke 12:35)

May I always be prepared to help others, Divine Savior.

The Torch of Faith

Donna Reed starred in classic films, such as *It's a Wonderful Life* and *From Here to Eternity*. But before she lived a financially comfortable life in Hollywood, she had seen her share of hard times and learned lessons on how to endure them.

In an essay for *Guideposts*, Reed recalled growing up on a farm in Denison, Iowa. Not only were times difficult because of the Great Depression, "on top of that came the drought that withered crops and parched the earth...[and] the wind that swept the dry topsoil into great, dark, choking dust storms."

Many families left, but Reed's father held on to hope, in part because of the messages he heard at their Methodist church every Sunday— messages like the passage from Isaiah 41, "When the poor and needy seek water, and there is none...I will make...the dry land springs of water."

Reed's family survived the Depression, and her father's example stayed with her. She said, "Faith and courage are like torches passed from old to young...With [God] we know that if we fail today, tomorrow offers its triumphs."

I the God of Israel will not forsake them. (Isaiah 41:17)

Help me transform tragedies into triumphs, Holy Spirit.

Forgiveness: A Gift We Give Ourselves

"Bitterness is unforgiveness fermented," writes Dr. Gregory Popcak in *Shalom Tidings* magazine. "The more we hold onto past hurts, the more we become drunk on our own pain, and the experience can rob us of the joy we can find in anything."

Dr. Popcak offers several suggestions for moving through bitterness, the first being, "Forgive." That doesn't mean you forget what was done to you or say you're okay with it: "According to Saint Augustine, forgiveness is simply the act of surrendering our desire for revenge...Forgiveness is the gift we give ourselves that enables us to stop picking at the scab and start making a plan for healing."

"Stop dwelling and retelling" is another recommendation. Dr. Popcak says, "It is fine to talk to people whom we think can help us heal the hurt, facilitate reconciliation, or help us rebuild our lives, but other than that, we should do what we can to stop dwelling on the story...The best course of action is to re-focus on what we can do today" to progress in our plan for healing.

Put away from you all bitterness. (Ephesians 4:31)

Grant me the grace to move past bitterness, Divine Healer.

The Positive Side of Getting Lost

GPS technology on our phones means we modern folks get lost a lot less than we used to. But Patheos.com blogger Rabbi Ben Greenberg doesn't think that's always a good thing.

He recalled a drive from Chicago to Pennsylvania to visit his girlfriend (now wife) when they were younger. He made it most of the way without any problems, but got lost on the local roads. That experience, however, prompted him to ask strangers for guidance, savor the smell of the farmland around him, and even pay a visit to the local homemade ice cream shop. In other words, he connected with new people and a new environment.

Rabbi Greenberg related this to the 40-year journey of the Jewish people after escaping from Egypt. God could have led them to the Promised Land more directly, but their comfort would likely have led them to forget Him and His words. Instead, God wanted "to imprint the Torah in their DNA so it could never easily be forgotten."

The lesson? "God purposefully took us the long way so we would learn to pay attention, to see the details, to not lose sight of the world around us and the bigger picture."

You led the people whom You redeemed. (Exodus 15:13)

Holy Spirit, lead me in the right direction.

A Perfect Heart

"He was born into this world with many complications but a perfect heart." That's how singer-songwriter Brooke White described her Uncle Kelly on her Facebook page following his funeral. He had lived to age 56 even though many predicted he wouldn't make it past his teens. Along the way, he embraced a childlike joy for life.

White recalled, "I know it was sometimes a challenge having a son and brother with special needs, but he was even more of a gift to us. [He] taught us to love everyone. He passed away peacefully with his family around him...And I'm certain my grandpa White was so excited to greet him on the other side.

"That's what kept getting me as I stood with my cousins and sibling around the pulpit...We're all in different places and phases, often believing different things, but we're linked. I looked around and thought: who will be beside us when we go, and who will be there to meet us on the other side? Family. Yes, it's complex. [I'm] not exactly sure how it works, but it does."

In My Father's house there are many dwelling places. (John 14:2)

Embrace my loved ones who have passed into eternal life, Savior.

A Jewish G.I.'s Unexpected Savior

In July 1944, Nazi doctor Edgar Woll amputated Army Private Adam Levine's right leg, and took his dog tags as well. In doing so, he saved Private Levine's life—twice.

The young Jewish-American soldier had been captured by the Nazis and sustained a severe leg injury during a battle in France. Dr. Woll stood over Levine and asked what the "H" on his dog tags meant.

As reported by Larry McShane in New York's *Daily News*, it identified his religion as Hebrew. Levine thought he was a goner. Instead, he awoke from surgery missing a leg and his dog tags, and found himself transferred to a POW camp until the Allies rescued everyone.

Dr. Woll, however, had left a note in Levine's pocket explaining why his leg needed to be amputated. The American also concluded that Dr. Woll took his dog tags to keep the other Nazis from identifying him as Jewish, thereby saving his life.

Levine, now age 89, never connected with Dr. Woll after the war, but he has become friendly with his widow and children, who have now come to see him as "our extended family."

Seek justice, rescue the oppressed. (Isaiah 1:17)

Inspire enemies to show each other mercy, Prince of Peace.

The Earliest Age

Cato the Elder, an accomplished orator and writer, was also a Roman statesman. When he was over 80 years old, he started to study Greek. Someone asked him why he began such a hard undertaking at his age. Cato answered, "It's the earliest age I have left."

Too many of us spend time thinking it's too late: too late to learn, too late to play, too late to change. Strangely enough, it's apparently never too late or too early to make excuses for ourselves.

Each day of your life brought you to where you are and who you are today. Take advantage of your past and learn from it. Then consider how you can best use today—and tomorrow.

The earliest age you have left is now.

Like a drop of water from the sea and a grain of sand, so are a few years among the days of eternity. (Sirach 18:10)

Holy Wisdom, help me to live every day to the fullest.

Hope is a World-Changing Force

Real hope isn't happy talk; it's a world-changing force born out of pain and sacrifice. Take, for example, filmmaker Jason DaSilva, who was diagnosed with an especially debilitating form of multiple sclerosis at age 25.

Despite the bad news, he mustered up the courage to turn the camera on himself. The result was the Christopher Award-winning documentary *When I Walk*, which provides a window both into his own battle with the disease and into the daily struggles of all people with disabilities.

The film also becomes a love story when DaSilva meets and marries Alice Cook, who gives his spirit a needed infusion of joy. Through triumphs and tragedies, they carry the cross of MS together, giving witness to the power of selfless love.

In addition, DaSilva created the website AXSMap.com, which maps and identifies the places in his native New York that are most accessible to people with disabilities. Volunteers around the globe have now done the same and added the results to the website, making DaSilva's mission truly world-changing.

Endurance produces character, and character produces hope. (Romans 5:4)

Through life's trials, Lord, may I retain my sense of hope.

Miss Sunshine: Teacher Extraordinaire

She's got the right name for the job!

That, in a nutshell, is the story of Stephanie Sun, a 26-year-old who teaches fifth grade at Achievement First Brownsville School in Brooklyn, New York. Sun absolutely loves what she does. Not only does she love it; she's darn good at it too—so much so that she beat out hundreds of other teachers to earn a coveted award.

Sun was one of four teachers across the country who won the 2015 Fishman Prize for Superlative Classroom Practice, which honors teachers working in high-poverty public schools. Keith Brooks, her principal, told the *Daily News* that Sun reminds him of the teachers who inspired him over the years.

Nor is that name out of place. She's known as "Miss Sunny" and "Miss Sunshine" around the building because of her enthusiasm for the job. Sun reveals that her passion for teaching never wanes: "I just know if I'm around kids, I'll always have the energy to keep going."

May my teaching drop like the rain, my speech condense like the dew. (Deuteronomy 32:2)

Each of us are teachers in our own ways, Lord. Help us to reflect Your truth and love always.

How Old Are You Now?

"Bacon makes everything better," reads a sign on Susannah Mushatt Jones's kitchen wall. It seems appropriate for a woman who eats bacon, eggs, and grits for breakfast every morning. And while you might think Jones's doctor would criticize her food choices, he'd have a tough time convincing her to change them at age 116. Yes, that's right: she's 116 years old.

As reported by *USA Today*, Jones was born in Alabama in 1899 and attended "a special school for young black girls." After graduating high school in 1922, she helped her family pick crops before moving to New Jersey and, eventually, New York for work. Her concern for others led her and "a group of her fellow high school graduates to start a scholarship fund for young African-American women to go to college."

Jones is now blind and hard of hearing, but she is revered in the Brooklyn public housing facility where she's lived for 30 years. While she credits her longevity to "lots of sleep," her family believe it stems from her loving and generous nature. Those are virtues that make it a joy to be alive at any age.

Do not cast me off in the time of old age. (Psalm 71:9)

Enkindle a generous nature within me, Holy Spirit.

A Lesson from the Saints

Over the past few years, five-time Grammy nominee Matt Maher underwent some changes in his life that made him reflect on the future of the Church, as well as the social issues prevalent in modern culture. He noted that "politics has poisoned, in some ways, people's day-to-day life, especially on the Internet."

Maher wondered how to navigate these troubled waters as a citizen and a Catholic. Ultimately, he realized there was a proven place to find the answers he was seeking: with the saints.

During an interview on *Christopher Closeup* about his album *Saints and Sinners*, Maher explained, "The saints found a way to stand for God, to stand for the Church, but also to love tremendously and love fiercely. In doing that, they elevated the conversation.

"That's what I feel needs to happen in the Church. We need a lot of young men and women to respond to the call of God—not get bogged down in a lot of the arguments that are happening, [but instead] focus our eyes back on Jesus and be amazing examples that can help re-elevate the conversation."

Here is a call for the endurance and faith of the saints. (Revelations 13:10)

Focus my eyes back on You, Jesus.

Grief as Part of Life

At some point in life we are bound to experience a deep grief over the loss of someone dear to us. Grief can be devastating, and recovery may take a long time. But we are not helpless in the face of grief. Grief can have its positive aspects.

There is an old Chinese proverb that says, "Without sorrows no one becomes a saint." A time of grief can be a period of personal growth. Edward Marham once wrote, "Only the soul that knows the mighty grief can know the mighty rapture." Grief can help us appreciate the joyous moments that much more.

When grief comes, don't try to run from it. Accept the support of family and friends, cry when you feel the need, but do your best to get on with your life. That's what God wants for you—to live fully each day you have.

He has borne our infirmities and carried our diseases...he was wounded for our transgressions, crushed for our iniquities, upon him was the punishment that made us whole, and by his bruises we are healed. (Isaiah 53:4-5)

Thank You, God's Suffering Servant, for taking my weaknesses and sorrows upon Yourself.

Aging with Purpose

Msgr. Gerald Ryan of St. Luke's Church in the Bronx passed away at age 93, but he chose to work to the very end. He was a priest who shunned the idea of retirement because he loved his ministry of serving God's people.

Before his death, Msgr. Ryan was interviewed by Pat McNamara for his book *New York Catholics*. During a *Christopher Closeup* interview, the author recalled the visit: "I was sitting in the rectory with a line of people waiting to see him. I remember talking to the secretary, Madeline, and I said to her, 'Have you known him long?' And she said, 'Oh yes, since we moved into the parish. He's like my dad.' He was like a father figure, a friend, a brother to the people of Mott Haven. He was known as the mayor of 138th Street."

McNamara points out, "Research has shown that people who keep doing meaningful work into their later years of life have a happier and fuller, more meaningful existence."

That philosophy worked for Msgr. Ryan, and it's a lesson we can all take to heart.

In old age they still produce fruit. (Psalm 92:14)

May I never lose my sense of God-given purpose, Lord.

Music Builds Bridges of Peace

Establishing peace and harmony between Israelis and Palestinians seems like an impossible task, but the Jewish, Christian and Muslim members of the YMCA Jerusalem Youth Chorus have done just that amongst themselves.

Founded by 25-year-old Yale University graduate Micah Hendler, the choir consists of 30 high school students from East and West Jerusalem, and includes both Palestinian and Israeli singers. As their website states, "Through music and dialogue, [they] are able to see beyond their differences and conflicts, and work together for peace in their community and beyond."

Miel de Botton, a London-based singer-songwriter, found herself so inspired by the chorus that she brought its members to England and performed with them.

She said, "I am so thrilled that these young men and women who are often raised in the mistrust of each other have found a joyous way of connecting through music. During the hostilities [of 2014], they braved huge obstacles to rehearse with each other. They did so even in the bunkers. I was moved to tears."

The Lord...give you peace. (Numbers 6:26)

Help me, Jesus, to love my neighbor.

Why Don't People Slow Down?

We live in a fast-paced world, but journalist Carl Honoré, author of *In Praise of Slowness*, points out that's not a good thing. The Londoner discovered this firsthand when he saw a book of one-minute bedtime stories in a store. At first, he thought this was a great concept, but then realized he wanted to rush through time with his son that he should be appreciating.

During an interview with *Costco Connection* magazine, he said, "The world is this huge buffet of things to do, and the natural human instinct is to want to have it all. [However], if you try to have it all, you will end up hurrying it all."

In fact, many people are aware of the negative effects of living life at breakneck speed, but still persist in doing so. Why?

Honoré explained that there's a bias against the word "slow." Many people think it means "lazy, stupid, unproductive, boring." In addition, stress can become addictive. He said, "A high-speed lifestyle is like a drug; it's where we're in fight-or-flight mode. It changes the chemistry of the body and brain."

So how can we learn to slow down? Honoré shares five tips tomorrow.

My peace I give to you. (John 14:27)

Grant me good judgment, Holy Spirit, on living well.

Applying the Brakes to a High-Speed Life

If you're living life at breakneck speed but want to apply the brakes, Carl Honoré, author of *In Praise of Slowness*, offers five suggestions in *Costco Connection* magazine:

- "Breathe. Slow, deep breathing reoxygenates the body, which slows the heartbeat and stabilizes blood pressure. When you feel panicky, stop for a moment and take a few deep breaths."

- "Speed audit. Stop and ask yourself if you're doing whatever you're doing too fast. If you are...work more slowly."

- "Downsize your calendar. Look at your schedule for the next week, pick the least important scheduled activity and drop it. This will take some of the heat out of that particular day."

- "Schedule unscheduled time. Block off two hours in your week when you don't plan anything. This will guarantee you some time when you can slow down to your own rhythm."

- "Find a slow ritual. [It should] act as your personal brake and help you shift into a lower gear. It might be gardening, reading, cooking, knitting, whatever."

Come to Me, all you that are weary...I will give you rest. (Matthew 11:28)

In life's slow moments, guide me toward Your peace, Jesus.

Sandals Lead to College

After graduating from the University of Missouri in 2008, Liz Bohannon traveled to Uganda to learn more about the lives of women living in poverty. She grew to love the women she met there, and decided to start a business that could help pay for their college education, which averages between $2,000 and $3,000.

Bohannon had always received compliments on the sandals she constructed in college: flip-flop bottoms tied around the foot with a decorative ribbon. As reported by Forbes.com, she hired three Ugandan women to make the sandals, then returned to the United States where she spent six months driving through the country convincing boutique owners to buy her product.

Bohannon chose the name Sseko for her company because it means "laughter" in the Ugandan language. By the end of the 2015 school year, she will have sent 60 young women to university. On Sseko's website, she explains, "We work (hard) and we laugh and we love and we learn. And every nine months, we let go and we send these incredible women off to pursue dreams of their own."

Your work shall be rewarded. (2 Chronicles 15:7)

Lead businesses to combine social justice with profit, Lord.

Why Election Day is a Tuesday

Ever wonder why elections are always held on a Tuesday?

It all goes back to 1845, when Congress decided that the election laws needed standardizing. That was, of course, the horse-and-buggy era, and according to a brief item in *The New York Times*, that had a lot to do with it.

It seems that just about everyone went to church on Sunday in those days, so Sunday was ruled out as a day to go the polls. Since many people traveled a great distance to cast their ballots, Monday was similarly the wrong choice for rural residents to get into town. And since Congress was eager to pick the earliest time in the week as Election Day, Tuesday it was, and remains so to this day.

But wait a minute; that was then and now is now. Doesn't it make sense to hold elections on Sundays, as many other nations do? Nope. According to a 2012 congressional survey, it wouldn't make much difference. Americans are used to Tuesdays as their Election Day—and it looks as if it's settled in for the long haul.

This was done by public vote of the city. (2 Maccabees 12:4)

May an informed conscience guide my vote, Father.

How to Be Likeable

If you've ever wondered what makes a person likeable, Dr. Travis Bradberry, author of *Emotional Intelligence 2.0*, shared his thoughts on the *Huffington Post* website:

- **They ask questions.** Instead of focusing on what they're going to say next (which is something a lot of people do instead of actually listening), they ask questions that let the other person know they've been paying attention.

- **They are genuine.** "No one likes a fake. People gravitate toward those who are genuine because they know they can trust them."

- **They don't pass judgment.** "Being open-minded makes you approachable and interesting to others. No one wants to have a conversation with someone who has already formed an opinion and is not willing to listen."

- **They don't seek attention.** "You don't need to develop a big, extroverted personality to be likeable. Simply being friendly and considerate is all you need to win people over."

Set the believers an example in speech and conduct. (1 Timothy 4:12)

Help me to be a channel of Your grace to others, Jesus.

Praying for a Soldier

Country singer Sunny Sweeney was walking through an airport when she noticed a young soldier with a backpack waiting to board a plane. A stranger walked up to him to thank him for his service and to ask if he could pray for his safety. The soldier agreed, and the two men bowed their heads and began saying a quiet prayer.

Sweeney felt overwhelmed with emotion. She took a picture of the two men praying, then wrote on Facebook, "I started crying, of course, just watching this nice end to a [stressful] day unfold on my 16-hour cross-country flight, but Americans never cease to amaze me. Beautiful. I would love for this picture to find its way to the man pictured here in uniform to show how many people are praying for you and wishing you good thoughts and safe travels."

As usually happens in these cases, Sweeney was soon connected to the soldier in question, Michael Barth of Washington, through the all-encompassing web of Facebook. He felt grateful to have a record of this unexpectedly beautiful memory in his life.

God is our refuge and strength. (Psalm 46:1)

Lead all military members home to their families, Lord.

Dog Tags and Grace

At the 2014 opening of the Dog Tag Bakery in Georgetown, Washington, D.C., *CNN* anchor Jake Tapper called its proprietors "a match made in heaven." It was a clever way to describe Jewish philanthropist Connie Milstein and Catholic priest Father Rick Curry, S.J., and their mission with the store, which is appropriately located on Grace Street.

Blogger Janet Donovan attended the grand opening and explained, "The Bakery was born out of [Milstein and Curry's] shared conviction that no veteran with disabilities who wants to work should be unemployed." The store's workers simultaneously take business and finance classes at Georgetown to prepare them for future employment.

One of those workers is Sedrick Banks, an Army veteran who sustained brain injuries in combat. He told the *Washington Post*, "I could go into all the training that Dog Tag has offered, but the biggest thing it's helped me with is transitioning from a wounded warrior back into society. It's helped me recognize my capabilities despite my injuries."

Give us this day our daily bread. (Matthew 6:11)

Focus our minds on our abilities, not our disabilities, Lord.

Circle of Life in Nursing Home

Sister Stephen Bloesl has created a unique environment at Villa Loretto Nursing Home in Mt. Calvary, Wisconsin. Not only is it a residence for seniors, it's a home for farm animals.

Filmmaker Carolyn Jones profiled the nun, who is also a nurse, in her Christopher Award-winning documentary *The American Nurse*. During a *Christopher Closeup* interview, Jones said, "[Sister Stephen] brings in baby goats, baby lambs, baby ducklings. You've got people here who sometimes can't remember their family members, but you put one of these brand new baby lives in their hands, and they just come alive!

"Not only that, she brings in young people from [a nearby town] that are in Social Services. Some of these kids have had rough beginnings, but she gives them a place to go for the weekend. They care for the animals, then take them to the residents, so they're dealing with the elderly. There's this circle of life happening underneath this one roof in Villa Loretto."

Jones hopes that Villa Loretto becomes a model for other nursing homes around the country.

Your faithfulness endures to all generations. (Psalm 119:90)

Bring together generations for their mutual benefit, Lord.

The Human Spirit Unleashed from Fear

In his Christopher Award-winning book *Fully Alive: Discovering What Matters Most*, Special Olympics Chairman Tim Shriver shares a picture of the Special Olympics floor hockey team from Afghanistan who have withstood a lot of adversity to participate in their sport.

On *Christopher Closeup*, Shriver explained, "We've had attacks on our program, had one of our buses bombed because, in some situations, we include girls in the program. In other situations, it's because people have antiquated beliefs that [those with intellectual differences] ought to be excluded.

"But there they stand. Their coaches risk their lives. They do it not for money. They go to institutions and orphanages...and bring soccer balls and joy and excitement. They say 'Come on out. We're gonna show your parents that you've got gifts.' And it's amazing what the human spirit unleashed from fear will do. Those are modern-day saints. They're not headline saints, but they're saints in the sense that they follow what I see as God's invitation to be unafraid to love without boundaries."

Perfect love casts out fear. (1 John 4:18)

Jesus, grant us the courage to fight for what we believe.

In Times of Mental Anguish

Many years ago, The Christophers published a prayer called "In Times of Mental Anguish" for people going through difficult times. That prayer is timeless, so we're sharing it again:

"God, sometimes I think physical pain is less hard to bear than mental suffering. A toothache or a broken leg is at least in one place. But anxiety or tension, guilt or indecision are everywhere at once—and nowhere.

"When Jesus said, 'Not My will but Yours be done,' did His pain go away? I don't think so. But I believe that You made it possible for Him to bear it.

"Do for me, Father, whatever it was You did for Him. As I try to imitate His fidelity to Your will, may I experience Your peace—the peace that, somehow, can exist in the midst of great suffering. Amen."

In everything by prayer and supplication with thanksgiving let your requests be made known to God. And the peace of God, which surpasses all understanding, will guard your hearts and your minds in Christ Jesus. (Philippians 4:6-7)

Give me the grace to deal with mental distress, Divine Healer.

Adoption Can Heal Society's Ills

"Adoption is a lot easier than people think it is."

So says Judge David Gooding of Jacksonville, Florida, who has finalized adoptions for close to 4,000 children. He also notes that adoptions benefit the world at large: "Permanent loving families are a solution to a lot of society's problems. Children who age out of foster care, instead of being adopted, are four times more likely to enter the adult criminal justice system and 17 times more likely to be homeless before the age of 21."

In September 2014, a Jacksonville family gave six kids the opportunity to defy those odds. Lisa Sheek and her husband adopted six children that they had been fostering—five boys and one girl. As reported by News4Jax.com, the group consisted of siblings from two different families. Now, they're all members of a single, happy family.

Sheek explained, "A lot of people think you won't love a child that's not a biological child as much as you do another child, but we love them just as much, the same...They are extraordinary and they are survivors and they are my heroes."

You have received a spirit of adoption. (Romans 8:15)

Lord, inspire society to become more open to adoption.

The Mother and the Ex-Con

While eating brunch in a Steubenville, Ohio restaurant with her husband and four kids, Maura Roan McKeegan heard the man behind hear use foul language. Calmly, she turned to tell him, "Please watch your language; we have children with us."

McKeegan was surprised to find the culprit was a huge man with "long, greasy hair" and a "scar beside his eye." Though taken aback by his appearance, she smiled and looked him in the eye. The man's foul mood changed into one of contrition, and he explained, "I'm sorry. I just got out of prison, and I forget how to act sometimes."

Reflecting on the incident in *Catholic Digest*, McKeegan wrote, "When I met that man's eyes, I understood that when we visit prisoners, we visit Jesus. I'd like to think that when I looked into his eyes, I visited him in the loneliness of his prison cell...But maybe it was the other way around. Maybe I was the inmate, locked in a world that doesn't give a cursing ex-convict a second glance. Maybe he was the one who came to visit me in that prison and show me the way out—the way that begins with looking into a person's eyes and seeing God inside."

I was in prison and you visited me. (Matthew 25:36)

Guide all prisoners to redemption, Lord.

Belief Can Change Your Brain

Are people born brilliant—or can they become brilliant through hard work? Science doesn't offer a definitive answer, but a recent study from Michigan State University shed light on the power of belief versus genetics.

As reported by *Science Daily*, the study found that "simply telling people that hard work is more important than genetics causes positive changes in the brain and may make them willing to try harder." Lead investigator Hans Schroder added, "In contrast, telling people that intelligence is genetically fixed may inadvertently hamper learning."

Author and counselor Dr. Greg Popcak commented on this study on his Patheos.com blog: "As St. Thomas Aquinas reminds us, 'Grace builds on nature.' The more we believe we can accomplish, the more we tend to accomplish—even in areas where nature might lead us to think differently if we let it...The more you believe in God's grace and your good effort, the more likely it is that you can become your best self in every area of your life."

Whatever your task, put yourselves into it, as done for the Lord. (Colossians 3:23)

May I never underestimate my potential, Creator.

After Arrest, Teen Saves a Life

After getting arrested by Fort Lauderdale, Florida police officer Franklin Foulks for violating juvenile probation, 17-year-old Jamal Rutledge might have felt justified in holding a grudge against him. Instead, the teen helped save the policeman's life.

As reported by *WTVJ*, Officer Foulks collapsed while processing Rutledge's arrest at the police station. Though he was handcuffed, Rutledge kicked the security fence and yelled for help until three nearby officers came running. They discovered that Officer Foulks's heart had stopped beating, so they administered CPR and also used a defibrillator on him—two actions that ultimately saved his life.

Doctors credited Rutledge's quick thinking with helping to save the day. The teen and the three responding officers were all honored by the community for their efforts.

Do not neglect to do good and to share what you have, for such sacrifices are pleasing to God. (Hebrews 13:16)

Prince of Peace, guide me always toward choosing what is right and good, even in the most difficult of circumstances.

The Simplicity of Stories

As children, we loved hearing stories. It's how we learned. That's also how Christ taught: by telling stories.

One day an eight-year-old girl told her grandparents about a man named John. Seems he was a righteous man who started each day with a simple prayer: "Good morning, Lord, this is John. Please be with me this day."

Eventually, on the day John was dying in his hospital bed, there came a voice only he could hear: "Good morning dear John, this is the Lord. Indeed I have been with you all days. And this day you shall be with Me—in Paradise."

And with that, the little girl told her grandfather, "Now I say it every day, Pop-Pop. 'Good morning Lord, this is Becky. Please be with me this day.'"

Simple stories, simple prayers, simple love. That is perhaps what it's all about in this world.

Say to the Lord, "My refuge and my fortress. My God in whom I trust."...He will cover you with His pinions, and under His wings you will find refuge. (Psalm 91:2,4)

Master Storyteller, be with me and bless me this day.

Dude of the Week

Others may come and go but Bruce Beck seems to go on forever. The popular New York sportscaster has been airing his reports for the NBC outlet there for years now, and, as they say, it's beginning to look like a steady job. His sportscasts are informative, he delivers them with authority and good humor, and he's always got a smile on his face.

Now we've found another reason why he's a number one choice. In his weekly Sunday media column in the *Daily News.* Bob Raissman gave his "Dude of the Week" award to Beck and his family for helping the hungry.

For 15 years now, on the day before Thanksgiving, Beck, his wife Janet, and their sons Jonathan and Michael have dished out meals for as many as 1,200 folks in need for St. John's Bread & Life soup kitchen. For their efforts, they were given the Johnny's Angel Award in Brooklyn last year. "This is a charitable experience," Beck said, "which has shaped our family's life in a big way."

Whoever has two coats must share with anyone who has none...whoever has food must do likewise. (Luke 3:11)

Father, may my family be shaped by simple acts of charity.

Grace and Lace

Five months into her pregnancy in 2010, Melissa Hinnant received the news that her daughter would be born premature and likely not survive. While doctors kept the mom-to-be in the hospital and worked to delay labor, she decided to sew a blanket for her baby girl. Two weeks later, the child was born, but as Hinnant says, "the Lord took her straight to heaven."

As devastating as this loss was, it inspired a love for sewing in Hinnant. When she made herself a pair of lace leg warmers, strangers stopped her on the street, asking where they could buy a pair. Hinnant made some more and put them up for sale online. She was shocked when she became overwhelmed with orders.

Hinnant started a company called Grace and Lace, which became so successful, she wound up on the TV series *Shark Tank* and garnered entrepreneur Barbara Corcoran as an investor. In addition, a portion of every sale goes toward building Angel House orphanages in India, where Hinnant once spent the summer working with "the poorest of the poor." And it all goes back to the baby girl whose short life led to an ongoing legacy.

Your pain will turn into joy. (John 16:20)

May the losses in my life make me more compassionate, Lord.

Wrong Number, Right Person

At 5 a.m., on the day before Thanksgiving, 2009, San Diego real estate agent Virginia Saenz received a voicemail from a wrong number. The caller was Lucy Crutchfield, who thought she was phoning her daughter and therefore left an emotional reassurance that she would be sending her the money she needed to buy groceries for her and her children. Another detail: Crutchfield said she would use her mortgage money to do so.

Saenz, a mother herself, felt compelled to help this poor woman and her daughter. She called Crutchfield back immediately, telling her to keep her money because she was going to pay for the cost of her daughter's grocery items.

Sure enough, the following morning, Saenz enlisted the help of her 14-year-old son, and the two wound up buying a sumptuous Thanksgiving feast for Crutchfield's daughter's family. Saenz told *NBC 7 San Diego*, "I helped somebody. I think it's what anybody would have done."

It is more blessed to give than to receive. (Acts 20:35)

God, may we never underestimate the value of giving.

Three Franciscans Buy a Bar

Three Franciscan friars bought a bar in Kensington, Pennsylvania, in 1979. That's not the opening line of a joke, but rather the origin of St. Francis Inn, which feeds approximately 400 of the area's poor residents every day.

As reported by LoyolaPress.com, Father Michael Duffy, OFM, the Inn's co-director, makes sure the facility feeds people's bodies and spirits. It only seats 48 people at a time, so visitors are served in shifts and assisted by a maître d', wait staff, and volunteers to ensure feelings of human dignity. Father Duffy says, "One of our guidelines says we don't seek to serve the poor, we seek to be the poor, and serve our brothers and sisters."

The Inn receives no money from the state or archdiocese, only private donors. And the staff never turns anyone away. If the food runs out, they'll at least "slap together some peanut butter and jelly."

At the end of the day, Father Duffy knows the Inn serves a higher purpose: "The crowning glory of our work is for people to feel loved by God."

If you offer your food to the hungry...then your light shall rise in the darkness. (Isaiah 58:10)

Help me play a role in nourishing the hungry, Father.

Take Stock of Your Blessings

Rachel Cruze is a popular author and speaker who teaches young people to be smart with their money. She's also someone grounded in gratitude, so it's not surprising that her favorite holiday is Thanksgiving. She explained:

"My parents declared bankruptcy the year I was born. Because of that, I learned a lot about contentment early in life. My parents helped me see the important balance between working hard and trying to be successful and being thankful for how far you've already come (and what you've already achieved). While there's nothing wrong with setting goals and moving forward...never take for granted what you already have.

"If you're at a point in life where being grateful doesn't just flow naturally, don't worry. You might have to take time to sit down and put conscious effort into thinking about everything you are thankful for...This Thanksgiving, I want to challenge you to truly reflect on everything important in your life. That way, when Christmas rolls around, you'll have a firm foundation on what matters and what doesn't."

Come into His presence with thanksgiving. (Psalm 95:2)

Heavenly Father, help me develop a spirit of gratitude.

All is Well

"All is well, all is well/Angels and men rejoice/For tonight darkness fell/Into the dawn of love's light."

Those are the opening lyrics of three-time Grammy Award winner Michael W. Smith's song *All is Well*, which is featured on his album *The Spirit of Christmas*. Though he co-wrote the song many years ago, it's a message that he returns to often for comfort—one that's even displayed in his parents' home because his father is now suffering from dementia.

During an interview on *Christopher Closeup*, Smith said, "Every day when I'm over [at my parents' house], I'll ask, 'Hey Dad, what does that say over the chimney?' My dad will say, 'All is well, all is well.' So that's sort of become our motto during this chapter of our lives. I watch my kids and grandkids get these magical, amazing feelings [about Christmas]. Then there's watching my mom and dad get old, so it's an interesting chapter. But God is good and all is well at the end of the day."

During life's most trying times, trust in God and believe that, in the long run, all shall be well.

The Lord is near to the brokenhearted. (Psalm 34:18)

Send Your grace to victims of dementia and their caretakers, Divine Healer.

Shoebox Stories

Alex was only seven years old in 1994, when the Rwandan genocide occurred. In 2014, he recalled his grandmother and uncle being murdered before his eyes, a bullet once missing his head by an inch, and people arguing over whether or not to kill his entire family. With his mother having already died of AIDS, he wandered in a state of destitution with other members of his family, until he was finally placed into an orphanage.

During his first year there, the charity Operation Christmas Child arrived, bringing the children shoeboxes filled with gifts. Alex said, "That box gave me joy when there was nothing left... As a seven-year-old, I needed to be reminded that someone still loved me, someone still cared."

In the video accompanying his essay at Shoebox Stories online, Alex walks the grounds of the orphanage where he grew up and joins in handing out shoeboxes filled with gifts to all the children. He says, "God knows their hearts. And God will just use that gift to go enrich them in the deepness of their hearts."

I know the plans I have for you, says the Lord... to give you a future with hope. (Jeremiah 29:11)

Lord, thank You for lighting our way with gifts of hope.

The Unsatisfied Longing

The season of Advent brings a reminder of the longings we all experience in our hearts, says Father Robert Barron, recently named auxiliary bishop of Los Angeles. In a reflection for his media ministry Word on Fire, he shared the following thoughts:

"I've always sensed that the Advent attitudes of waiting, expecting, hoping and anticipating somehow speak to the deepest desires of our heart. That is probably because our whole existence here below is characterized precisely by these attitudes.

"The world is filled with wonderful things and experiences—deep joys and satisfactions. But we all know that nothing here finally satisfies us.

"No matter how much we know, we want to know more; no matter how much we love, we want greater love; no matter how much beauty we attain, we sense that there is a perfect beauty that we haven't seen. 'O come O come, Emmanuel, and ransom captive Israel.' That great Advent hymn catches our ache. As we move into this season of anticipation, allow that ache to develop, preparing you for the satisfaction that will arrive only in Christ."

Prepare the way of the Lord. (Isaiah 40:3)

Fulfill my deepest longings, Prince of Peace.

"Only" a Drop in the Ocean

Some problems, like poverty, seem so immense there's a tendency to question the value of one person's contribution. However, Mother Teresa of Calcutta, when asked about the work of her religious community, said, "What we are doing is just a drop in the ocean. But if the drop was not in the ocean, I think the ocean would be less because of the missing drop."

Others have expressed similar sentiments. Lutheran theologian and Biblical scholar Albert Schweitzer said, "Each of us can do a little to bring some portion of misery to an end."

There are personal rewards in doing each small good deed. Kahlil Gibran wrote: "In the joy of little things the heart finds the morning and is refreshed."

Finally, when your efforts seem insignificant, remember the words of St. Madeleine Sophie Barat, "Nothing that can please the heart of our Lord is small."

The kingdom of heaven is like a mustard seed that someone took and sowed in his field; it is the smallest of all the seeds, but when it has grown it is the greatest of shrubs and becomes a tree. (Matthew 13:31-32)

Jesus, remind me daily to love You in small, ordinary deeds as well as in great ones.

Surprising Shoppers at Christmastime

In December 2014, Father Jim Sichko of St. Mark's Church in Richmond, Kentucky, received a check for several thousand dollars from an anonymous donor. Along with the check came a note asking him to "pay it forward."

Therefore, Father Jim, who often preaches about the importance of giving back, picked a day where he would perform random acts of kindness in various places.

As reported by *WKYT TV*, he paid the bills of people shopping in local grocery stores, filling up their tanks at the gas station, and picking up food from the McDonald's drive-thru. He even stood in the mall and handed out $100 bills to Christmas shoppers. The reaction in most places was shock—though it was a happy kind of shock.

Father Sichko hopes his surprise gifts bring joy to their recipients and inspire them to be generous to others in return.

Those who are generous are blessed, for they share their bread with the poor. (Proverbs 22:9)

Guide me in being generous to others, Divine Savior, whether it be financially or via my time and talents.

Powerful in Their Simplicity

Christopher literature, including our News Notes and the book you're reading right now, is popular nationwide, so we often donate these items to various diocesan prison ministries.

Longtime Christopher friend Sister Rosemary Dowd, who ministers to inmates in Chicago, wrote us a note saying: "This week, an older man asked if I could give him anything to read that would 'lift his spirits.' I was able to find a [*Three Minutes a Day*] book to bring him. They are so popular that they aren't always available...I am so grateful for the goodies you send. The men love everything I put out for them when we have our twice-weekly Communion services. [They say], 'If it is from The Christophers, it is good!'"

Another supporter named Marylou recently wrote to us saying, "Thank you for your faithfulness in sending the Christopher News Notes. They transform what is 'ordinary' to 'extraordinary,' from the secular to the sacred. They are powerful in their simplicity."

Thanks to you, dear reader, we can continue sharing our messages of hope with people everywhere.

God...leads the prisoners out to prosperity. (Psalm 68:6)

Touch the hearts and souls of all prisoners, Redeemer.

Being the Uncool Dad

Matt Archbold is an old-fashioned dad who's protective of his children, so when his 15-year-old daughter wanted to go over to a friend's house, she knew he would want to speak to her father first. She made the video call on her iPad, then handed it to Archbold, hoping the conversation would achieve her desired result. It didn't.

As Archbold recalled in *Catholic Digest*, the other father told him that everything would be fine, that kids should have their own space, and that it's important to be a "cool dad" because "studies have been done" showing that being strict with kids will result in their being rebellious when they go to college.

Archbold's daughter heard all this and simply shook her head knowing that she wouldn't be going to her friend's house that night. Instead, Archbold took her to the movies and bought her ice cream afterwards. "This makes me a cool dad," he joked.

"No," she responded. "You could never be a cool dad. And that's a good thing. I don't want a cool dad. You don't even care about being cool. That's what makes you a dad."

Train children in the right way. (Proverbs 22:6)

Lord, help fathers be more concerned with their children's well-being than with being popular.

Get Your Anti-Stress Kit Here!

Could you use an anti-stress kit? The inspirational newsletter *Apple Seeds* suggests these easy-to-find items:

- **Rubber Band:** to remind you to stretch your new ideas and your mind to new limits so you will continue to grow and reach your potential.
- **Candy Kiss:** to remind you that everyone needs a hug, kiss, or word of encouragement every day.
- **Life Saver:** to remind you to think of your peers as your life savers. Care about each other and help each other through the stressful times that occur in life.
- **Eraser:** to remind you that we all make mistakes and with an eraser they can be erased, as can our human mistakes be overcome.
- **Toothpick:** to remind you to pick out the good qualities in others and yourself—and to be tolerant and accepting of the differences of others.

Do not worry about anything, but in everything by prayer and supplication with thanksgiving let your requests be made known to God. (Philippians 4:6-7)

When stress gets high, remind me to trust in You, Lord.

The Lonely Patient

A young woman visited her mother in the hospital. An elderly woman, near 90 years old, was in the same room. She never had visitors, and spent most of the time sleeping.

The young woman arranged for her mother to have television. As it was being installed, the elderly woman asked for service, too. The technician said he couldn't provide it unless someone paid for it.

The young woman followed him outside the hospital room, and paid for several days' service. Her mother objected, thinking that her daughter shouldn't get involved and that she shouldn't throw away money like that.

The next day the elderly woman was sitting up alert, watching television, laughing and animated. When the young woman's mother left the hospital, she gave the elderly woman her slippers and a brightly colored scarf for her hair. These small but simple good deeds brought new life to a woman who had felt abandoned by the world.

Be kind to one another, tenderhearted. (Ephesians 4:32)

You are present in all of us, Master. Show me how to share Your goodness with others.

Waiting with Patience

The late priest and author Henri Nouwen once wrote the following words about practicing patience. They're especially appropriate during the Advent season:

"How do we wait for God? We wait with patience. But patience does not mean passivity. Waiting patiently is not like waiting for the bus to come, the rain to stop, or the sun to rise. It is an active waiting in which we live the present moment to the full in order to find there the signs of the One we are waiting for.

"The word patience comes from the Latin verb 'patior' which means 'to suffer.' Waiting patiently is suffering through the present moment, tasting it to the full, and letting the seeds that are sown in the ground on which we stand grow into strong plants. Waiting patiently always means paying attention to what is happening right before our eyes and seeing there the first rays of God's glorious coming."

May you be prepared to endure everything with patience, while joyfully giving thanks to the Father, who has enabled you to share in the inheritance of the saints in the light. (Colossians 1:11-12)

I struggle with impatience, Lord. Send me Your peace.

A Vietnam Vet's Change of Heart

When he was a 19-year-old soldier in Vietnam, Bill Fero lost his legs to a booby trap. That incident, along with three years of agonizing hospitalization, turned him into a physical and emotional wreck. His body was in a wheelchair while his mind festered with hatred for all things Vietnamese.

When offered the chance to house refugees from that country, he took the opportunity for revenge. Instead of extending a helping hand to families desperate to escape their ravaged country, he made them his servants.

They received no kindness, just orders to clean, cook and do all of the chores on his small farm. The immigrants cheerfully accomplished all the Herculean labors without complaint. Their continuing kindness melted his anger.

In time, he welcomed and aided more than 40 families. He now collects medical supplies for Vietnam.

Probably the last thing you expect from someone you wrong is kindness. Maybe that's why it can change lives.

Love your enemies and pray for those who persecute you. (Matthew 5:44)

Lord, give me a forgiving heart.

An Adult's Belief in Santa Claus

As a child, author and theologian G.K. Chesterton received Christmas presents from Santa Claus, like most children. As an adult, his belief in Santa grew even stronger. Why? He wrote:

"Then I only wondered who put the toys in the stocking; now I wonder who put the stocking by the bed, and the bed in the room, and the room in the house, and the house on the planet, and the great planet in the void.

"Once I only thanked Santa Claus for a few dollars and crackers. Now, I thank him for stars and street faces, and wine and the great sea. Once I thought it delightful and astonishing to find a present so big that it only went halfway into the stocking.

"Now I am delighted and astonished every morning to find a present so big that it takes two stockings to hold it, and then leaves a great deal outside; it is the large and preposterous present of myself, as to the origin of which I can offer no suggestion except that Santa Claus gave it to me in a fit of peculiarly fantastic goodwill."

Great is our Lord, and abundant in power; His understanding is beyond measure. (Psalm 147:5)

Lord, help me to see life's deeper spiritual truths.

What Goes Around...

A postal clerk in Indianapolis made a discovery about her customers and co-workers—and her own human nature.

A newspaper editorial charged that her branch had "the rudest clerks in town." That statement made the clerk angry. "I was rude to people because they were rude to me," she said. "What goes around comes around."

Then she wondered what would happen if she treated others with courtesy. Would that come around, too?

So, she made an effort to get to know customers' names. The clerk began to smile and ask how they were doing. Even a man known for his grouchiness eventually became a favorite customer. All the clerks began to make an effort. Everybody reaped a reward of cheerfulness.

And it all started with one woman who decided that "what goes around comes around" can be good news.

Show every courtesy to everyone. (Titus 3:2)

May Your courtesy to me remind me to be courteous to others and to myself, God.

The Rose-Tinted Glasses of Grace

2014 was a dark and difficult year for Father Bob Colaresi, O. Carm., Director of the Society of the Little Flower which honors the life of St. Thérèse of Lisieux.

After suffering a fall, he experienced severe back pain and numbness in his legs, which required painful physical therapy. "And following my typical Sicilian pattern of punishing with silence," wrote Father Colaresi, "I stopped praying and communicating with God and Thérèse."

His condition had improved by Christmas Eve mass, and when he was holding a baby boy as part of his homily, something deep within his spirit awakened to the new life all around him.

He realized, "There were so many other ways new life was blossoming and happening that I was not being attentive to because I was listening to echoes of death, disappointment, and darkness. Instead of looking at life through dark sunglasses that blocked the sunshine, our souls need the rose-tinted glasses of grace to see what truly is, as God sees."

Each of us was given grace according to the measure of Christ's gift. (Ephesians 4:7)

When hope is hard to see, open my eyes with Your grace, Lord.

Regaining Your Soul for the Holidays

Martina McBride is a country music superstar who often shares words of hope through her songs. Her brother Steve also has a way with words, but he uses them on his blog, Crossroads.

Before the 2014 Christmas season, he shared the following reflection to get readers into the right frame of mind:

"We like to think that today's society is the most advanced, most intelligent, and most enlightened, but in reality it's far from it. In our little world of five-minute sound bites, zombie-like iPhone staring and game playing, we have lost our very souls. We have lost the art of good conversation and, most important, the art of listening and observing...We haven't got time to talk. We have things to do or places to go only to discover one day that we had all the time in the world and the ones [we] really want to listen to are now gone.

"So do yourself a favor this holiday season. Slow down. Look. Listen. And laugh. Remember the holidays gone by, tell your kids to go outside and not blend in with the couch. Count your blessings."

My soul thirsts for God. (Psalm 42:2)

Free me from distractions and open my eyes to the love that surrounds me, Prince of Peace.

Young and Old: A Good Match

DOROT—a word which means "generations" in Hebrew—is a Jewish social services organization in New York City that helps seniors feel less isolated. And thanks to one generous 14-year-old boy, some of these seniors can now play chess.

Zachary Targoff had started coming to DOROT as part of its ministry which connects teens with senior citizens. He found he enjoyed playing chess with 91-year-old Herman Bonze, and thought it would be great to teach everyone the game. "We used the money I got from my bar mitzvah to fund this program," Targoff told the *Wall Street Journal*.

"I'm thrilled you're teaching me chess," said one 97-year-old lady as she made an incorrect move of her chess piece. It didn't seem to matter whether she would ever become proficient. She was enjoying the new challenge. And Targoff still plays with his original partner, Bonze, whose daughter said that when her father is playing chess "he's at his best."

Are there ways you can nurture intergenerational connections in your community?

When you turn gray I will carry you. (Isaiah 46:4)

Father, bring young and old together in a spirit of fun.

What God Wants for Christmas

In 2014, country music singer Darius Rucker debuted a new Christmas song that deserves to become a classic. It's called *What God Wants for Christmas*, and it's grounded in the religious meaning of the holiday, delivering a perfect sacred message in what can seem an increasingly secular season.

Here are some of the lyrics: "I wonder what God wants for Christmas, Something that you can't find in a store. Maybe peace on Earth, no more empty seats in church, Might be what's on His wish list...What do you give someone who gave His only Son? What if we believe in Him like He believes in us? I wonder what God wants for Christmas, What might put a smile on His face. Every Bible with no dust, the devil givin' up, Might be what's on His wish list."

When you're making up your Christmas list this year, don't forget to include God, who gave us the greatest gift of all.

For God so loved the world that He gave His only Son, so that everyone who believes in Him may not perish but may have eternal life. (John 3:16)

Jesus, Your Divine Presence is the greatest gift of all at Christmas and always.

Pope Francis's Secrets to Happiness

Pope Francis is a popular pope with both Catholics and non-Catholics alike. His friendly, generous, humble nature seems to extend to everyone he meets. In an interview published in the Argentine weekly *Viva*, Pope Francis offers tips on living that have personally brought him great happiness:

- **Give of yourself to others.** "If you withdraw into yourself," the pope says, "you run into the risk of becoming egocentric."
- **"Proceed calmly" through life.**
- **Develop "a healthy sense of leisure."** More children and even adults need to plug in less and talk, read and play more.
- **Sundays should be a holiday, reserved for time with family.**
- **Find innovative ways to create jobs for young people.**
- **Respect and care for the nature that surrounds you.**
- **Try to banish negative thoughts and actions from your life.**
- **Respect the religious beliefs of others.**

Trust in the Lord, and do good. (Psalm 37:3)

Father, our source of true happiness lies in Your love.

Heisman Trophy Winner Supports Students

Football star Marcus Mariota has begun paying it forward, big-time. The 2014 Heisman Trophy winner, whose quarterbacking skills led the Oregon University team to the national championship, established the Marcus Mariota Scholarship Fund to aid incoming freshmen in financial need at his alma mater, Saint Louis School in Honolulu, Hawaii.

The scholarship will be awarded each year to a new or returning student entering the ninth grade, and will be applied to the student's tuition for four years. *The Hawaii Catholic Herald* reported news of the fund's establishment.

"Saint Louis School and my family made me who I am today," Mariota said. "I want future generations of student-athletes in financial need to know they can become the best they can be in a strong, supportive environment."

Mariota was the nation's number-two pick in the National Football League draft, chosen by the Tennessee Titans.

The advantage of knowledge is that wisdom gives life to the one who possesses it. (Ecclesiastes 7:12)

Lord, help student-athletes find the right balance between education and sports.

The Poinsettia That Led to Healing

Christmas brings with it the expectation to be joyful, but in 1999, Joanne Huist Smith was anything but. Her husband Rick had died a few months earlier, leaving her and their three kids—Megan, Nick, and Ben—emotional wrecks. Smith herself was angry at God and wanted nothing to do with Christmas.

Her road to healing began on December 13 as Smith rushed out of her Bellbrook, Ohio house to warm up her car because she needed to drop the kids off at school. She nearly knocked over the poinsettia sitting in front of the door. Attached was a note that read, "On the first day of Christmas your true friends give to you one Poinsettia for all of you."

During a *Christopher Closeup* interview about her book *The 13th Gift*, Smith admitted that if Megan hadn't been with her, she likely would have thrown the flower away. But Megan, who Smith says has Christmas in her heart, was thrilled that someone had left it for them. Smith assumed it was just a one-time act of kindness, but then gifts started arriving every day.

More of the story tomorrow.

Every perfect gift...is from above. (James 1:17)

Help me to be an anonymous blessing to someone in need, Lord.

Simple Gifts Exert Profound Influence

When anonymous gifts started arriving at her house every day, Joanne Huist Smith says that she felt "bamboozled by unwanted acts of kindness." But soon, she admitted, "my attitude began to change: going from anger to 'who's doing this' to 'thank goodness they're doing it for us.' The people who left those gifts knew a lot about grief and they knew that one gift wouldn't be enough. And they were right."

Even though the items they left were simple things like red bows and wrapping paper, the gifts exerted a profound influence over the Smith family.

Smith said, "Trying to figure out who had left [them] for us, who cared enough to come day after day after day, that got us sitting down at the dinner table and the breakfast table talking about it—and that was something we had not done for a while."

The Smiths found a renewed sense of life, love, and purpose that Christmas, prompting them to do for others what was done for them.

The conclusion of the story tomorrow.

A gift in secret averts anger. (Proverbs 21:14)

Move me toward love and service this Christmas, Father.

Pay It Forward at Christmas

Since that Christmas in 1999, Joanne Huist Smith has made her peace with God while anonymously helping other families in the same way that hers was helped.

Her experiences have also qualified her to give some advice to others who are enduring grief during the holiday season: "I really believe that no matter your situation, there are others who need help more. Find them, help them. Don't sit at home and be unhappy. Get out in the world."

In addition, by writing *The 13th Gift*, she hopes to inspire selflessness in others: "I would hope that more people will help me to pay it forward this holiday season and all year, to start a movement where we all become gift-givers in our own special way: smiling at strangers, giving a gift to someone you don't like, visit a family like ours who's suffered a lot. I guarantee that the reward for your actions and the good feeling you get in return will far outweigh your effort. That's my Christmas wish."

Do not withhold good from those to whom it is due, when it is in your power to do it. (Proverbs 3:27)

Inspire in me the same giving spirit with which You sent us Your Son, Father.

The Unfriendly Neighbor

In his book *God Delights in You*, former Director of The Christophers Father John Catoir shared a letter he received about reaching out to the seemingly unlovable. It read:

"Some years ago, I had a very unfriendly neighbor with a most unattractive personality. In her final illness, I went to see her in the hospital. She had lived alone, never married, and had no friends. In this first visit she looked so frightened and alone that my heart went out to her. It seemed to me that this was a woman who had never been loved. I did everything I could to convince her that I cared for her. It wasn't much, but I held her hand, smoothed her forehead and spoke to her in a loving tone of voice. I really did care.

"During that time I could sense her responding with love and almost joy. She only lasted about two weeks. My hope has always been that through my love, she came to know God's love. I've done many things in my life that required more self-sacrifice, but somehow this one stands out, possibly because there was no pride or self-interest involved."

Love is patient; love is kind. (1 Corinthians 13:4)

Help me be a friend to the friendless, Prince of Peace.

The Lottery Man's Kindness

On Christmas Eve, 2002, a stressed-out Christine Basney was raising four children, studying in college, and working in a small Michigan country store when Richard Heath walked in.

Heath bought a scratch-off lottery ticket and won $100. He asked for the winnings in two $50 bills, then gave one to Basney and one to her co-worker as holiday gifts.

More than 10 years later, Basney, now a registered nurse, walked into a patient's room to introduce herself. She was surprised to see it was Heath. They both recognized one another.

"As soon as I saw him, my eyes welled up with tears....I told him that Christmas 2002 had been the roughest ever for me, and $50 went a long way. I was deeply honored to be caring for him," she wrote for the *AARP Bulletin*. "I never forgot how kind total strangers can be, and I have tried my hardest to be as kind as the lottery man."

What does the Lord require of you but to do justice, and to love kindness, and to walk humbly with your God? (Micah 6:8)

May we keep reminding ourselves of how very important acts of kindness are, Jesus.

Diamonds are a Child's Best Friend

Here's a heart-warming little Christmas story that comes to us courtesy of The Salvation Army, by way of "Mighty Quinn," who writes a column each day for New York's *Daily News.*

At Boston's North Station, it seems, the Army's bell-ringers found an unusual item in one of the red donation kettles they tend to each day—a diamond engagement ring. The ring turned out to be an anonymous gift from a widow, given in memory of her late husband.

She asked that the ring be sold in order to buy toys for needy children so they'd have some gifts from Santa under the Christmas tree.

"I'm hoping there's someone out there," she wrote in a note found with the ring, "who's made lots of money this year and who will buy the ring for 10 times its worth. After all, there's no price on love or the sentimental value of this ring. May everyone have a Merry Christmas, Happy Holidays and a Happy New Year!"

Sell your possessions, and give the money to the poor, and you will have treasure in heaven. (Matthew 19:21)

Inspire the 'haves' to share with the 'have nots,' Jesus.

A Prayer for God's Light to Shine

Today, we'd like to share a prayer by St. Thomas More: "Father in heaven, you have given us a mind to know You, a will to serve You, and a heart to love You. Be with us today in all that we do, so that Your light may shine out in our lives.

"We pray that we may be today what You created us to be, and may praise Your name in all that we do. We pray for Your Church: may it be a true light to all nations; May the Spirit of Your Son Jesus guide the words and actions of all Christians today. We pray for all who are searching for truth: bring them Your light and Your love.

"Give us, Lord, a humble, quiet, peaceable, patient, tender and charitable mind, and in all our thoughts, words and deeds a taste of the Holy Spirit. Give us, Lord, a lively faith, a firm hope, a fervent charity, a love of You. Take from us all lukewarmness in meditation, dullness in prayer. Give us fervour and delight in thinking of You and Your grace, Your tender compassion towards me. The things that we pray for, good Lord, give us grace to labour for: through Jesus Christ our Lord. Amen."

I am the light of the world. (John 8:12)

Sustain my faith and shine Your Eternal Light through me, Heavenly Father.

Subway Conductor Says, "Smile!"

Riding the train to work one December morning, The Christophers' Director of Communications Tony Rossi and his fellow passengers heard a unique message from the subway conductor over the loudspeaker:

"A dangerous situation our city is facing has to do with a diminishment of social skills. We forget to do simple things like smile at one another and say hello. It seems if we did more of that, there would be less hatred and violence in our world. So as we enter this season of love and joy, don't forget to smile."

On The Christophers' blog, Rossi wrote, "His message made me smile both because of its content and the novelty of it. But as I looked at the people around me, no one made eye contact so maybe it didn't get through to everybody. Then again, it didn't need to. I'm sure that message will stick with a few of the hundreds of people on that train so several seeds of kindness were planted. That's a pretty good result for a morning's work. And considering that Mother Teresa once said 'Peace begins with a smile,' this subway conductor is in good company."

A glad heart makes a cheerful countenance. (Proverbs 15:13)

May I radiate Your joy to all I meet, Jesus.

Drivers Happy to Get Pulled Over

Police officers in Lowell, Michigan, pulled over quite a few cars in December 2014. As they took the drivers' licenses and registrations, the officers casually asked them what their kids wanted for Christmas. Listening in via radio were the police department's own "Santa's helpers" at a nearby store, where they would buy the gifts the people were talking about, wrap them, and rush them over to the traffic stop to surprise the drivers.

The drivers, of course, were thrilled. "This turned my bad day into a good one," said one woman who unwrapped a radio-controlled truck for her son. Another mom with her arms full of new toys asked Officer Scot VanSolkema, "Can I hug you?" Then she added, "I'm not getting a ticket, right?" Officer VanSolkema joked, "I can give you one if you want."

The project was funded by *UP TV*, recorded, and posted online as a four-minute video. At the end, a message reads: "While we don't encourage minor traffic violations, it's important for police departments to take the time to show their citizens just how much they care." No doubt the citizens of Lowell will never forget that Christmas.

So deeply do we care for you.
(1 Thessalonians 2:8)

Bring peace to all communities, Father.

The Legacy of Family

Patheos blogger Deacon Greg Kandra's sister-in-law gave her father some precious Christmas gifts in 2014: pictures of his grandmother Agnes and a few paragraphs telling her story. Agnes was widowed at an early age and raised nine children on her own. She supported her family by teaching school and through the generosity of family, friends, and members of her parish church.

Deacon Kandra's father-in-law wept at the legacy he held in his hands, a legacy that had helped make not only his life possible, but also that of his children and grandchildren.

The Deacon concluded, "In one way or another, we are all here because of those who came before us...They sailed on ships to a vast stretch of uncharted earth where they plowed fields, built cities, mined coal, dug wells, forged steel, and paved roads. They fell in love, raised families, and saw in this land a place of possibility. Some did it against incredible odds. Whisper a prayer tonight for these good souls, most of whom we may never have met or known. Their legacy is a gift that keeps on giving."

We will tell to the coming generation the glorious deeds of the Lord. (Psalm 78:4)

Instill me with appreciation for my family history, Lord.

God Grant Us Grace in All Our Days

The Darkest Midnight is an old Irish Christmas carol from the Wexford singing tradition. It was re-recorded in 2014 by U2 lead singer Bono for Michael W. Smith's album *The Spirit of Christmas.* The lyrics reflect the true meaning of this holy day, and serve as a beautiful Christmas reflection:

"The darkest midnight in December/No snow nor hail nor winter storm/Shall hinder for us to remember/The babe that on this night was born./With shepherds we are come to see/This lovely infant's glorious charms./Born of a maid as the prophets said/The God of love in Mary's arms./Ye blessed angels join our voices/Let your gilded wings beat fluttering o'er/While every soul set free rejoices/And every one now must adore./We'll sing and pray that God, as always/May our friends and family defend./God grant us grace in all our days/A Merry Christmas and a happy end."

Do not be afraid; for see — I am bringing you good news of great joy for all the people: to you is born this day in the city of David a Savior, who is the Messiah, the Lord. (Luke 2:10-11)

May I always remember and cherish the true meaning of Christmas, Savior.

What is Christmas?

An old Christopher friend, the late William Arthur Ward, once shared these thoughts on the true meaning of Christmas:

"Christmas is more than a time of music, merriment and mirth; it is a season of meditation, mangers and miracles.

"Christmas is more than a time of gaiety, greenery and gifts; it is a season of wonder, worship and wise men.

"Christmas is more than a time of festivities, family and friends; it is a season of generosity, gladness and gratitude.

"Christmas is more than a time of carols, cards and candy; it is a season of dedication, direction and decision.

"Christmas is more than Santa, stockings and surprises; it is Christ, care and compassion."

During this busy and joyful season, take the time to silently reflect on the deeper truths of Christmas. They may bring you more peace than the biggest gift under the tree.

A Child has been born for us, and a son given to us...and he is named Wonderful Counselor, Mighty God, Everlasting Father, Prince of Peace. (Isaiah 9:6)

Help us find You, Child Jesus.

Stretch Your Way to Success

The world-renowned actress Helen Hayes used to tell an intriguing tale about her early days in the theater. A producer told her she could be great—if only she were four inches taller.

"So," said Hayes, "I was pulled and stretched until I felt I was in a medieval torture chamber. I gained nary an inch—but my posture became military. I became the tallest five-foot woman in the world."

Her new posture gave Hayes a new attitude. "My refusal to be limited enabled me to play Mary of Scotland, one of the tallest queens in history."

It's a good story to remember when facing any limitation. Try to change, to stretch your limits. But if that isn't possible, consider stretching your own attitude. It could be your key to success.

Though I walk in the midst of trouble, You preserve me against the wrath of my enemies; You stretch out Your hand, and Your right hand delivers me. The Lord will fulfill His purpose for me; Your steadfast love, O Lord, endures forever. (Psalm 138:7-8)

Help me, Creator, to move past the limitations the world has set for me—or that I have set for myself.

Honesty — and a Second Chance

Tom and Pauline Nichter of California were homeless and jobless when they found a wallet containing a large amount of cash. Rather than taking the money for themselves, the Nichters returned the wallet to its rightful owner.

They were rewarded for their honesty. The local police gave them $300 and strangers sent donations. An elderly couple gave them a check for $2,400, the amount in the wallet.

The couple, who had been out of work for a year, were about to give up hope when all of this happened. They were overwhelmed by the kindness of strangers.

As Pauline Nichter said, "I can't believe this. All we did was what we were brought up to do—to be honest. We're getting our second chance, and God, it feels good."

Honesty is not a quality of character that becomes disposable in hard times. If you are a person of integrity, it is who you are—and how you live every day.

Trust in the Lord, and do good; so you will live in the land, and enjoy security. (Psalm 37:3)

I want to turn from all that keeps us apart, Savior. Make me the person You want me to be.

Time to Write a 'Thank You' Note

"Never forget the apostolate of the short note," someone once said, and an important mission it is. It came true not long ago for Father Joe Breighner, who writes a column for the *Catholic Review*, Baltimore's archdiocesan paper.

The writer of the note said to Father Joe: "After all these years, I have the cassette tapes from your show back in the 1980s. I can honestly tell you that I would not be writing this had you not been in my life to help me through the teenage years. My heart has always had love and gratitude for you in my life. You were my hero, and through you I understood faith and love."

Quite a note, which Father Joe quoted in his column. He wrote quite a reply, too: "Each of you reading this column is a hero to someone, perhaps to many someones. As parents and grandparents, as aunts and uncles, as brothers and sisters, as teachers and helpers, you have impacted others in ways you may never know this side of heaven…A thank-you note has power that we never know."

I do not cease to give thanks for you as I remember you in my prayers. (Ephesians 1:16)

May I always take the opportunity to say 'thank you,' Lord.

You Are at the Top When...

Motivational speaker and author Zig Ziglar often shared thoughts about achieving success. Here are some of his ideas from a list called, "You are at the top when..."

- You clearly understand that failure is an event, not a person; that yesterday ended last night, and today is your brand new day.

- You know that success (a win) doesn't make you, and failure (a loss) doesn't break you.

- You are mature enough to delay gratification and shift your focus from your rights to your responsibilities.

- You know that failure to stand for what is morally right is the prelude to being the victim of what is criminally wrong.

- You are pleasant to the grouch, courteous to the rude, and generous to the needy.

- You can look back in forgiveness, forward in hope, down in compassion, and up with gratitude.

- You stand in front of the Creator of the universe and He says to you, "Well done, thou good and faithful servant."

Commit your work to the Lord, and your plans will be established. (Proverbs 16:3)

May I define success by Your divine standards, Lord.

Positive Beginnings

There are lots of superstitions about New Year's Day. Many of them involve foods that are supposed to bring good luck for the coming year.

For instance, Pennsylvanians have a tradition of eating pork and avoiding turkey on New Year's Day. The reason is, a turkey scratches backward, but a pig roots forward representing a forward-looking approach to the new year.

Even if superstitions about food have no real basis, the value of a forward-looking approach is unquestionable.

Instead of dwelling on past mistakes or bad luck, we need to make constructive plans for the future. A positive outlook coupled with determination are more important than "luck" in shaping our lives.

New Year's Day may be associated with making resolutions, but any day is a good time for a fresh start if we choose to make it so.

You have been born anew, not of perishable but of imperishable seed, through the living and enduring word of God. (1 Peter 1:23)

Renew us each day, Holy Spirit.

A Most Human Prayer

The Jewish Theological Seminary of America took a full-page ad in the *New York Times* a while back to say Happy New Year to people of all faiths or no faith.

It contained some memorable words on prayer: "Start small. Bless one moment for what it brings you. Say one ancient prayer, link yourself with continuity and eternity. Fill one silence with your end of the conversation. No one can do this for you; it belongs to you."

Is there a believer from any faith who could not profit from these suggestions? A non-believer who could not find food for thought? Only we humans can believe, can pray, can speak—with words or with silence. Start a conversation with God. Enter His presence.

Prayer is a truly human activity that links us with the Divine. It's the perfect way to begin the year.

[Jesus] would withdraw to deserted places and pray. (Luke 5:16)

Lord, teach me to welcome You, to listen to You, to speak with You each day.

Also Available

We hope that you have enjoyed *Three Minutes a Day, Volume 50*. These other Christopher offerings may interest you:

- **News Notes** are published 10 times a year on a variety of topics of current interest. Single copies are free; quantity orders available.

- **Appointment Calendars** are suitable for wall or desk and provide an inspirational message for each day of the year.

- **DVDs** include classic Christopher films, clay-animated Christmas stories, and Father John Catoir's reflections on making prayer simple and joyful.

- **Website—www.christophers.org**—has *Christopher Closeup* radio programs; links to our blog, Facebook and Twitter pages; a monthly *What's New* update; and much more.

For more information about The Christophers or to receive News Notes, please contact us:

> The Christophers
> 5 Hanover Square
> New York, NY 10004
>
> Phone: 212-759-4050/888-298-4050
> E-mail: mail@christophers.org
> Website: www.christophers.org

The Christophers is a non-profit media organization founded in 1945 by Father James Keller, M.M. We share the message of personal responsibility and service to God and humanity with people of all faiths and no particular faith. Gifts are welcome and tax-deductible. Our legal title for wills is The Christophers, Inc.